Situational Leadership® II Model

Leadership Styles

Development Levels

Self
Leadership
and The
One
Minute
Manager

Revised and Updated Edition

Books by Ken Blanchard

One Minute Mentoring (with Claire Diaz-Ortiz), 2017

The New One Minute Manager (with Spencer Johnson), 2015

Legendary Service (with Kathy Cuff and Vicki Halsey), 2014

Trust Works! (with Cynthia Olmstead and Martha Lawrence), 2013

Great Leaders Grow (with Mark Miller), 2012

Lead with LUV (with Colleen Barrett), 2011

Who Killed Change? (with John Britt, Pat Zigarmi, and Judd Hoekstra), 2009

The Secret (with Mark Miller), 2009

The Fourth Secret of the One Minute Manager (with Margret McBride), 2008

The One Minute Entrepreneur (with Don Hutson), 2008

Lead Like Jesus (with Phil Hodges), 2006

Customer Mania! (with David Novak), 2004

The On-Time, On-Target Manager (with Steve Gottry), 2004

Full Steam Ahead! (with Jesse Stoner), 2003

High Five! (with Sheldon Bowles, Don Carew, and Eunice Parisi-Carew), 2001

Gung Ho! (with Sheldon Bowles), 1998

Everyone's a Coach (with Don Shula), 1995

Raving Fans (with Sheldon Bowles), 1993

The One Minute Manager Builds High Performing Teams (with Donald Carew and Eunice Parisi-Carew), 1990

The One Minute Manager Meets the Monkey (with William Oncken, Jr.), 1989

The Power of Ethical Management (with Norman Vincent Peale), 1988

Leadership and the One Minute Manager (with Patricia Zigarmi and Drea Zigarmi), 1985

Putting the One Minute Manager to Work (with Robert Lorber), 1984

The One Minute Manager (with Spencer Johnson), 1982

Books by Susan Fowler

Why Motivating People Doesn't Work . . . and What Does, 2014

Achieve Leadership Genius (with Drea Zigarmi and Dick Lyles), 2011

Leading at a Higher Level (with Ken Blanchard et al.), 2009

Good Leaders, Good Shepherds (with Dick Lyles, Tim Flannigan, and Drea Zigarmi), 2007

The Team Leader's Idea-a-Day Guide: 250 Ways to Make Your Team More Effective Every Day of the Year (with Drea Zigarmi), 1997

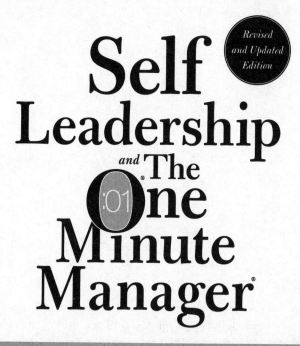

Self Leadership and The One Minute Manager

Revised and Updated Edition

Gain the Mindset and Skillset for
Getting What You Need to Succeed

Ken Blanchard

Susan Fowler

Laurence Hawkins

WILLIAM MORROW
An Imprint of HarperCollins*Publishers*

Grateful acknowledgment is made to Bristol Park Books for permission to reprint "The Business Card Trick" from *The Mammoth Book of Fun and Games* by Richard B. Manchester. Copyright © 1976 by Hart Publishing Company, Inc.

HarperCollins books may be purchased for educational, business, or sales promotional use. For information, please email the Special Markets Department at SPsales@harpercollins.com.

Library of Congress Cataloging-in-Publication Data has been applied for.

ISBN 978-0-06-269867-4

17 18 19 20 21   DIX/LSC   10 9 8 7 6 5 4 3 2

To my mother, Dorothy Blanchard,
who taught me how to take control of my own life before
someone else did.
—KEN BLANCHARD

To my wonderful parents, Phyllis and Dick,
who helped me realize the magic of self leadership
by encouraging my curiosity, independence,
and love of learning.
—SUSAN FOWLER

To my three daughters, Genevieve, Ashley, and Juliet,
with the fondest hope that they may be beneficiaries of
these self leadership concepts and tools and immerse
themselves in the good life.
—LAURENCE HAWKINS

Contents

Introduction by Ken Blanchard   xi

1   Do You Believe in Magic?   1
2   People Are Not Mind Readers   15
3   Elephant Thinking   23
4   Cycles of Power   37
5   Diagnose Yourself   57
6   Getting What You Need   71
7   Running Together   83
8   No Excuses   103
9   One Minute Magic   121

Appendix: The Business Card Trick   131
Acknowledgments   135
About the Authors   137
Services Available   141

Introduction

Today it's imperative that people become self leaders—individuals capable of setting priorities, taking initiative, and solving problems independently.

In the old days, command-and-control managers often made all the decisions and told people what, when, and how to do things. We now know that this management style can erode a healthy sense of autonomy and dampen people's initiative, creativity, and sense of well-being.

The nature of 21st-century work requires a more collaborative working environment. Advances in technology are decentralizing the workplace. For example, more people are working virtually and using cloud-based tools to move projects forward. Things are changing so rapidly that direct reports often know more about their work than their managers do.

In today's collaborative, decentralized workplace, it's essential that individuals become proactive contributors rather than reactive order-takers. For things like sales campaigns and customer service initiatives to succeed, they must be supported by people skilled in proactive self leadership.

First published in 2005, SELF *Leadership and the One Minute Manager* introduced a proven path to empowerment in the guise of a fun-to-read parable. In the increasingly fast-paced world of work, this updated edition is more relevant than ever.

If you are an individual contributor, this book will show you how to be proactive about getting the help you need in order to succeed. If you are a manager or executive, this book will teach you the fundamentals about developing self leaders.

Our research shows that when individual contributors and managers align around self leadership, both become more engaged and produce better results. As a result, customers are happier and organizations become more profitable. In fact, a culture of self leadership is the hallmark of great organizations. In these companies, leadership is happening everywhere, not just in the C suite.

So enjoy this story. As you'll soon discover, self leadership is not a rare ability reserved only for the supermotivated and highly gifted people of the world. It is a mindset and skillset that can be learned—and taught.

Self
Leadership
and The
One
Minute
Manager

1

Do You Believe in Magic?

Steve cleared his throat and looked around the conference room table. "Welcome, everyone."

After months of preparation, this was the moment he had been working so hard for—his first ad campaign presentation. And he was more than a little nervous. The ten men and two women sitting before him were his clients, and they would decide if his campaign was acceptable for the upcoming year.

Steve distributed spiral-bound copies of the campaign proposal to the eleven vice presidents and then handed one to Roger, the president of United Bank.

"I'd like to begin by reviewing our budget." Steve directed their attention to the projector screen, where he presented the budget amounts allocated to design, production, and media buys. He discussed his media recommendations and the rationale behind each one. Next, he explained the underlying thinking that had gone into the creative part of the campaign.

"Any questions?" Steve asked.

Around the table, people shook their heads. Steve sensed they were just waiting to see what the campaign was going to look and sound like. "All right, let me move on to the creative approach we're recommending."

Directing the presentation from his laptop onto the projector screen, Steve revealed storyboards for the proposed television commercials. Next, he showed preliminary print ads and direct mailers. Finally, he read the radio ad scripts out loud.

When his presentation came to an end, Steve took a deep breath and waited to hear what they thought.

At first, no one spoke. The silence stretched uncomfortably.

Finally, one of the VPs said, "You took a much lighter approach than I thought you would, but maybe that's good—it projects a friendly bank."

Another VP spoke up: "You've obviously put a lot of time and effort into this campaign."

After another awkward silence, all heads turned to Roger, the bank's president.

"This is garbage," Roger said.

Stunned, Steve went blank. He simply didn't know how to respond. He nodded his head as though he were trying to shake out a thought. "I guess we've missed the mark," Steve finally managed. "I'll go back and talk to the creative team. I'll be back in touch next week."

Steve didn't remember how he got to his car. He found himself driving—but not back to the agency. There was no way he could face his team. Thank heaven his boss, Rhonda, was out of town. He needed to find a place where he could be alone and think. He also needed a good cup of coffee. Driving through an unfamiliar neighborhood, he happened upon a place called Cayla's Café. He went in hoping to find relief.

He gazed around the bookstore café with its solid wood tables and matching heavy wood chairs. It was a very different place than the high-tech chrome and high energy of the ad agency. He found solace in the cavelike coolness, and was warmed by the smell of coffee.

What had gone wrong? How did things get so far off track?

Steve ordered a mocha and let the warmth of the mug seep into his palms. After this latest fiasco, he was sure to be fired. As he thought about it, he was surprised he had gotten this far.

Five years before, Steve had felt as though he'd won the lottery. Rhonda, cofounder of the Creative Advertising Agency, had hired him straight out of college with a degree in marketing. He'd taken an entry-level position and quickly worked his way to lead production manager in charge of several large accounts. Last year he'd served as coproducer of the industry's awards program for outstanding ad campaigns.

Four months ago, Steve felt flattered when Rhonda gave him the opportunity to bypass the typical career path as a junior account exec on a larger account and take the account exec role on a small but well-regarded account—United Bank. Rhonda told Steve that she wanted to empower him, and that this was the perfect time to do so.

Steve saw his promotion as his chance to prove himself. If he could make a mark with United Bank, he could soon take on the more prestigious, big-budget accounts.

Or so he had thought. Now his confidence was shattered and his future in question. The meeting had unnerved him. The more he thought about the bank president's reaction, the angrier he got.

In a blinding flash, Steve realized the real source of his failure—it was Rhonda. She'd abandoned him! Where was she when he needed her and when everything was falling apart? Why hadn't she warned him that the client was a nightmare, that the copywriter on his team was a whiner, and that the art director was an egomaniac? Rhonda was the one person who could have saved him from this humiliation, but instead, she'd "empowered" him. He had trusted her and she'd fed him to the wolves.

Now that he had proved to be a failure, Steve was sure Rhonda would fire him. He decided to beat her to the punch. She wouldn't fire him—he'd quit! He pulled out a yellow legal pad and pen to begin drafting his resignation letter.

He was just writing the first sentence when his attention was drawn to a group of young children trying to muffle their laughter as they gathered under a rustic sign claiming the area as Cayla's Magic Corner. He watched as a small, vibrant woman moved in front of the children and sat down on a simple wooden stool facing them. She rested her forearms on her thighs and leaned close to them. Not saying a word, she gazed intently at each child. Steve could have heard a pin drop.

"I am Cayla," she said softly, enunciating each word as though revealing a great mystery. "And I am a magician."

She told them about an old Indian mystic who taught her the art of mind over matter. To demonstrate, she pulled out two rubber bands, entwined them, and pulled and tugged to show that they could not be separated.

Milking the tale for all it was worth, Cayla claimed she could separate the two bands using only the power of her mind—and then she did so. The children roared their approval. It was truly magical. Steve regained his focus and went back to writing his resignation letter, losing track of time.

"Did you enjoy the magic?"

The voice jolted him out of his deep concentration. Steve looked up and saw Cayla standing beside him. He rose awkwardly and held out his hand.

"Sorry, I hope you didn't mind—it was fun to watch you. You're a good magician. My name is Steve."

"Mind? Not at all," the woman said as she returned the handshake. "I was hoping you'd join in. My name is Cayla."

"I like that name."

Cayla smiled. "Thank you. My parents loved the name because it means 'empowered' in Hebrew. Maybe that's where I get my magical powers," she said with a laugh.

Steve gave her a wistful smile. "I remember when I believed in magic. I also remember how disappointed I was when I realized there was no such thing as magic. But don't get me wrong—I still appreciate the skill behind the tricks."

"You don't believe in magic," she said with a sigh. "Too bad, because it looks as though you could use some."

Steve was too startled to reply. He'd had no idea he was that transparent. Cayla pulled a chair over from the adjacent table and sat down, motioning for Steve to sit as well.

"Listen," she said, gazing at Steve with the same intense eye contact she'd given the children earlier. "You are obviously a businessman, yet here you are in this bookstore at midday. You've barely touched your coffee and scone. Something is bothering you."

Encouraged by her compassionate smile, Steve told Cayla his sad story, beginning with his excitement and pride at being given his own client after less than two years with the company.

"But it wasn't long before my dream turned into a nightmare," he explained. "Even in the initial client meetings we struggled to establish an advertising budget. I had developed media and production budgets in the past, but I couldn't tell the client what was appropriate for them. Nothing in those early meetings confirmed their good first impression of me or the agency—and it went downhill from there.

"There was no budget, no goals, and no strategy. I didn't know how to direct my creative team without an agreed-upon advertising strategy. The client drove me crazy—no one could agree on anything!"

Cayla nodded thoughtfully as she listened to Steve pour out his side of the failed client relationship. "What about your creative team? Did they help?" she asked.

"Oh, they're another story. Creative people are worse than spoiled children. I tried to give them direction, but it was like herding cats. When they asked for more specifics, I tried to explain that the client couldn't agree on a strategy. But it all fell on deaf ears. They just told me that it was my job to figure out what the client wants, even if the client isn't sure! How am I supposed to do that? Finally, I demanded they come up with something—anything—that I could show the client. So they did."

"I'm afraid to ask . . ." Cayla's statement trailed into silence.

"That's why I'm here. It was a fiasco. The client hated it. Heck, I hated it. I knew it was no good, but it was all I had." Steve was holding his head in his hands as though the burden was too much to contemplate. "I'm sick to death of the whole creative process. I'm not creative, so I have to depend on my team, and they're totally undependable! It puts me in a no-win situation. How am I supposed to manage the creative process when I'm not creative?"

Cayla pressed on. "So what do you do now?"

"I'm writing my resignation letter," Steve said matter-of-factly.

"Hmm," Cayla said thoughtfully, "Quitting?"

"Yeah, before I get fired," Steve responded.

"Why don't you go to your boss for help?" Cayla asked.

"It's too late. What can Rhonda do now? We're probably going to lose the client—and she'll blame me, even though it's not my fault."

"Whose fault is it?" Cayla asked.

Steve shook his head, feeling even more betrayed by Rhonda. "Isn't it obvious? When Rhonda abandoned me, it all fell apart. Now I've even lost confidence in the things I used to do well, like budgets, media, and production. I didn't realize advertising is such a dog-eat-dog world. It's not like I thought it would be," Steve lamented.

"Just like the magic," Cayla interjected. "You loved magic when you were naïve and could suspend your disbelief. But now you are disillusioned by it, because you realize there's a trick behind the magic."

"I'm not sure there's any trick behind succeeding in this business. If there is, no one has bothered to show me," Steve said defiantly.

"If you don't mind me saying so, it sounds as though you're full of excuses—a poor victim of circumstance."

Cayla's comment struck Steve as harsh and he replied defensively. "What do you mean, 'a victim of circumstance'?"

"I mean a person who refuses to accept responsibility for the situation he's in. It's easier to blame everyone else around you, rather than accepting responsibility for yourself," Cayla replied without apology.

"Hold on. You can't blame me for what's happened. Rhonda's expectations were unfair. I didn't get the support I needed from her or from the creative team—I could go on and on," Steve asserted.

"So," continued Cayla, "Rhonda should have known better than to delegate the account to you and give you the freedom to do your job, right?"

Steve was a little annoyed—and surprised—at the turn the conversation had taken. Yet in his heart he knew she had a point.

Cayla's eyes filled with empathy and in a soothing voice she said, "Right now you're feeling confused and unsure. You sense there's some truth in what I'm saying, but buying into it would mean that *you* must be the responsible one—not Rhonda, your client, or your temperamental creative team. Somehow that doesn't feel fair. You're even feeling a little scared."

Steve stared at Cayla, wondering how this woman could know all that. It was as though she could read his mind.

"Let me explain," Cayla offered before Steve could ask. "I can't read your mind. As a magician, I'm a master of observation, although right now you're not all that hard to read."

Cayla looked straight into his eyes. "Steve, years ago I was in a boat very similar to the one you're sinking in. Fortunately for me, I met a wonderful guy known as the One Minute Manager. What he taught me created such a miraculous change in my life that I call it magic. I'd like to pass that magic on to you."

"Magic?" Steve asked incredulously. "I think I need more than smoke and mirrors to deal with this mess!"

"It isn't in smoke and mirrors," Cayla said flatly. "The magic comes from self leadership."

Steve was quick to reply. "Leadership might work for the One Minute Manager, but I'm not a manager—let alone a famous one. I'm a lowly account executive with a manager who doesn't support me—not when it counts."

Cayla lifted an eyebrow. "That's how it looks from where you're sitting now—which is on the pity pot." She smiled as she said it, and Steve couldn't suppress a chuckle. "You have to turn the problem upside-down," Cayla continued, "so that you're the one on top. It's time to stop looking for excuses and start proactively leading yourself."

"Thanks for the pep talk, but I don't believe in pop psychology or magic bullets," Steve said glumly.

"I need you to suspend your disbelief, as you did when you were a child watching magic and believing. I need you to believe in the magic of self leadership," Cayla said.

Steve half-grinned as he asked, "All right, what's the trick?"

"Actually, there are three tricks. I'll share them with you when you are ready."

"How do I know when I'm ready?"

"You are ready for self leadership when you accept responsibility for your own success."

"You mean I have to stop blaming Rhonda, my creative team, and the client and look in the mirror at what I did or didn't do to succeed?"

"Yes," she replied. "You need to stop thinking of empowerment as a four-letter word and realize that it is a grand opportunity. You need to start taking the lead to get what you need."

There was a long pause as Steve pondered Cayla's challenge. Finally, he said in a soft voice, "I think I get it. Rhonda empowered me to do a job, and I failed to take the initiative and responsibility for succeeding in it. I played the role of a victim. The problem with being empowered is that when things go wrong, you have no excuses. There's no one to blame but yourself."

"Here's the truth of it: There's only power in empowerment if you are a self leader." Cayla waited for Steve's eye contact. "Remember:

*

*Empowerment
is something
someone gives you.
Self leadership
is what you do
to make it work."*

*

"I obviously failed the self leadership test. But I can't afford for my résumé to reflect that I was fired—even if I deserve it. I've got my resignation letter almost finished. I need to get it to Rhonda before she gets back from her trip," Steve declared.

"Whoa!" Cayla held up her hand. "There you go again with the pity party! What happened to self leadership?"

"That's what I'm doing," Steve argued. "I'm taking the initiative and quitting!"

Cayla shook her head and laughed. "There are times when quitting is appropriate, but this isn't one of them. Why are you so convinced you don't have a chance? No one has actually warned you, have they?"

"No, but I know what she will think," Steve said defiantly.

"Steve, is this statement true or false? 'People are not mind readers, so it is unfair to expect them to know what you are thinking.' "

"True, with you being the possible exception," Steve said with a smile.

Cayla smiled back. "So if Rhonda can't possibly know what you are thinking, how are you so sure you know what she is thinking?"

"You have a point," he said.

"What about this statement? 'It is in my own best interest to take responsibility for getting what I need to succeed in my job.' "

"I guess the responsibility is mine," Steve agreed hesitantly, "but I'm not sure what to do."

"Follow me," Cayla said.

2

People Are Not Mind Readers

Steve followed Cayla to the back of the store and saw her slip through a door with a small nameplate bearing her name. When he reached the doorway of Cayla's office, he stood transfixed. Inside was a forest of shelves, boxes, barrels, trunks, and cabinets stuffed with magic paraphernalia. It was an enchanted place, not because of the things in it, but because of the feeling he got when he entered the room.

Cayla went over to an old, oak filing cabinet labeled "Magic of Proactive Self Leadership." She opened the top drawer, rifled through files, and pulled out a sheet as she exclaimed, "Abracadabra!"

Steve laughed despite himself, caught up in Cayla's joy of finding a single piece of paper.

"Your homework for this afternoon," she said, handing him the sheet.

Instructions : Rank the following workplace motivators according to their importance to you. Place the ranking (one through ten) beside the motivator with one being most important, through ten being the least.

_____ Interesting work

_____ Full appreciation of work done

_____ Feeling of being "in" on things

_____ Job security

_____ Good wages

_____ Promotion and growth within the organization

_____ Good working conditions

_____ Personal loyalty to employees

_____ Sympathetic help with personal problems

_____ Tactful disciplining

"After you've ranked the motivators, then ask at least five of your coworkers for their rankings. Bring it all back to me tomorrow and tell me what you learned."

"Is this a trick?" Steve asked skeptically.

"It's the beginning of one!" Cayla said enthusiastically. "What you learn from this assignment will reinforce what you learned today and introduce you to the first trick of being a self leader."

"Okay, I'll go along with this for now—but I'm not saying I won't quit. I have until my boss gets back at the end of the month to make up my mind." Saying the words filled Steve with foreboding. He had never left a job under negative circumstances. "If you don't mind me asking, what's in this for you?"

Cayla smiled. "Remember the One Minute Manager guy I told you about? After he got me out of my mess, I asked him how I could repay him for all his insight and help. He told me that the one thing I could do was pass on the learning to others.

"Besides," she continued with a wink, "my life purpose is to be a magician. You are giving me an opportunity to do magic."

"I guess I *could* use a little magic right now," Steve admitted. "I'll see you tomorrow."

•   •   •

Steve arrived back at the agency and ducked into his office when one of his team members happened by. He knew he'd have to face his failure tomorrow at the scheduled meeting, but he wasn't ready to talk about it just yet.

Using his printer, he scanned the sheet Cayla had given him and e-mailed the electronic version to five coworkers: Rhonda's assistant, Phyllis; a young account executive named Grant; his buddy in the mailroom, Mike; his favorite tech, Skye; and Ricardo, the senior partner on his floor. The e-mail went out with the following message:

> I need your help for a study I'm conducting. Could you take a few moments to fill out this survey and drop it by my desk on your way out today? It's "homework" I have to turn in tomorrow.
>
> Thanks,
> Steve

He then took a couple of minutes to rank his own sheet.

Just before the end of the day, Phyllis dropped by his office.

"I finished your survey," she said. "It's very intriguing. I'll be interested to hear what you learn when your study is complete."

Before Steve could respond, Grant popped his head in. Handing his survey back to Steve, he said, "No offense, but I don't see how this study is going to prove anything. I mean, it's pretty obvious that interesting work is what really motivates people."

"Actually, job security is what's important to me," said Phyllis.

"No way!" said Skye, who had overheard the conversation as she entered Steve's office. "It's all about good working conditions!"

Mike arrived moments later and argued that having his work appreciated was what motivated him most.

The group began a raging debate over the most important motivators. Each had their own rationale for their ranking. As the noise level escalated, Ricardo came out of his office to investigate.

"What's going on?" he asked.

"It's about the survey I sent you earlier today," Steve said, handing him a copy.

The Madison Avenue–dressed exec glanced at the list and said, "Oh, that. It's pretty obvious that people are motivated by good wages. All of you have asked for more money in the past, so I assume that's what motivates you."

The group stood in quiet surprise. None of them had mentioned good wages in their top three choices. As people shared their top motivators with Ricardo, his mouth dropped open.

"I can't believe I've worked with this team for years without knowing what's really important to you."

Steve said, "That's the point of this exercise! Each of us has different things that motivate us. Grant's creativity demands interesting work. Phyllis values security, probably because she's raising a young family. Plus, what motivates you today may change tomorrow."

Steve looked at the mailroom clerk. "For example, when Mike's kids get older and he's thinking about sending them to college, good wages may go to the top of his list."

"Okay," Grant allowed, "maybe different things motivate each of us. Is that the point?"

Steve thought about his discussions with Cayla. She'd said this survey would reinforce what he'd learned earlier and lead to the first trick of self leadership. Suddenly, the dots connected in Steve's mind.

"The point is, our bosses are not mind readers!" he exclaimed. "How in the world can we expect them to understand what motivates each of us? It's not fair to them—or to us."

Feeling true excitement about his insight, Steve looked at each of his colleagues one by one and declared:

✹

*"Ultimately, it's in
your own best
interest to accept
responsibility
for getting what
you need
to succeed in
the workplace."*

✹

3

Elephant Thinking

The next morning Steve pulled up to Cayla's Café and parked in a spot just outside the storefront. A little chime rang as he entered the door—a melodious signal to the clerks that someone might need their help. As he ordered his mocha, he heard someone whistling across the room. It was Cayla, who motioned for him to join her.

Steve grabbed his mug and moved toward Cayla. She disappeared behind a bookcase, but he followed the whistling and found her digging through a desk in her little office.

"So," she began without looking up, "how did the assignment go?" She continued to search the drawer.

"I did the survey, and I think it underscored what you said yesterday about people not being mind readers. I'm not sure where it's leading, but it taught me something."

"What did you learn from the survey?" Cayla asked as she pulled a pair of scissors from a tangle of rubber bands and paperclips.

"It wasn't so much the survey, but the discussion it generated. It became obvious that no boss can know and provide the motivation that every individual needs. Each of us has a different motivation for doing what we do, so it is up to us to take initiative for creating a professional environment that works for us," Steve concluded confidently.

"Well done," Cayla said with a smile. "You have proved ready to accept the responsibility of self leadership. It's time to learn the first trick of a self leader." Cayla picked up her scissors and led Steve to a table nestled among the bookshelves. "What other insights did you have about being a self leader?"

"I don't know if this will make sense, because I usually need time to process things," Steve said.

"Go ahead," Cayla encouraged.

"It has to do with my whole way of thinking about the workplace—things I have believed since I started working, even as a kid. Up until yesterday, I thought my boss should know what I need and give it to me. But that's not how it works. I wonder what else I have wrong."

"Do you have a business card?" Cayla asked.

"Sure," Steve said. He pulled a card from his briefcase and handed it to her. "I apologize. I should have given one to you yesterday."

"It's not for me—it's for you. It's a challenge." Cayla held the standard-size business card in both hands, turning it over several times as though to be sure there was nothing abnormal about it.

She slid the scissors in Steve's direction and ceremoniously laid the business card down on the table. "Take these scissors and cut a hole from the card large enough to go around your head. By the way, a hole is a space surrounded by continuous paper—no gaps or breaks, or joining ends."

Steve looked at her as though she were crazy. Cayla sat silently, waiting.

"I know you said you were going to teach me some magic, but I don't have time for games, Cayla. My job is in jeopardy."

Cayla replied, "I know you think you don't have time for this. You can't imagine how it could be useful or relevant and besides, it's just a trick, right?"

"Now that you mention it, I hate parlor tricks—I've never been any good at them. I've lost more money in bars than you can imagine. Some people just have a knack for this kind of thing—I don't."

Cayla nodded. "Elephant thinking."

"Excuse me?"

"You've limited yourself based on your past experiences," she said. "When they begin to train an elephant, they chain the baby elephant's leg to a pole in the ground. The baby elephant wants to get away. He pulls and tugs, but he can't escape—the chain is too big and the pole is too deep in the ground. So he stops trying. As he grows up, he just assumes he can't get away.

"Today he's a six-ton elephant. He could sneeze and pull out that chain—but he doesn't even try. Trainers say they can put a piece of string around that six-ton elephant's leg and he won't break away."

"So you're saying I'm like that elephant?" Steve frowned. "That because I've failed in the past I don't even try anymore?" Hearing the words out loud, he realized there was some truth in what he was saying.

Cayla smiled. "You have just tapped into the first trick of a self leader."

Steve perked up. "Really?"

"Yes. It's those kinds of assumptions that limit you every day. They're called ***assumed constraints***."

"What's a consumed restraint?" Steve asked.

She laughed at his mangled terminology, then clarified:

✶

*"An **assumed constraint**
is a belief
that limits your
experience."*

✶

"Okay, I understand that I have assumed constraints about this scissors-and-card trick, but what's that got to do with my work situation?" Steve asked.

"You are assuming you know what Rhonda, your team, and your client think and feel. You are assuming you can't be successful in your role at work. You need to knock it off."

"This is depressing," Steve said.

"It could be inspirational," Cayla countered.

"Too bad I don't have your powers of observation. Then I'd know what everybody is thinking and I wouldn't jump to assumed constraints so often," Steve said.

"Being able to read people is a gift—but the greater gift is to know your *own* mind."

Steve winced. "Yeah. That's a definite challenge."

Cayla nodded. After a pause she said, "I have to go, but while we're on the subject of challenges, are you ready to cut a hole from your card big enough to go around your head?"

Steve took the scissors and picked up the card. To his astonishment, his business information was no longer on the card. Instead were the words:

The First Trick of a Self Leader:
CHALLENGE
ASSUMED
CONSTRAINTS!

He glanced up to commend Cayla on her sleight-of-hand, but she was gone. With an amused smile, he shook his head. Looking at his watch, he realized he should be gone, too. In less than an hour he was due back at the office for his dreaded postpresentation team meeting.

Steve arrived back at the agency just in time to do some last-minute preparation. He'd been procrastinating, not sure how to tell the team members that their efforts had been rejected by the client. He knew they would look to him for answers, and he didn't have any.

The team—the creative guys, production assistant, and media buyer—filed into the conference room to hear what United Bank had thought of the presentation. They must have sensed it wasn't good news. Without much chatter they took their places and waited for Steve to begin the meeting.

Steve began on a positive note. "United Bank acknowledged and appreciated the hard work that went into the campaign."

Peter, the art director, interrupted. "You don't have to butter us up, Steve. They must not have bought it or you would have said something before now. What did they say?"

Steve took a breath. "They said it was garbage."

Even Peter had no comeback.

Steve spoke into the silence. "I think we all would agree that it wasn't our best work. I don't have any answers right now, but I do have an apology."

He noticed he had everyone's complete attention. "My presentation was fine, and the effort you gave was fine. What didn't work was the lack of an agreed-upon budget and overall strategy. You can't create something in a vacuum—and for that, I accept responsibility."

"Well, they aren't the easiest people to work with," Maril, the media buyer, offered.

Alexa, half of the Peter and Alexa creative team, said, "They're bankers! What do they know about creative work? They probably wouldn't know good creative work from a hole in the ground!"

Steve was floored by the team's comments. All this time he had assumed their disdain was for him, when actually it was the client that they had issues with. At first he was relieved, but then he realized that their perceptions came from the negative energy he'd shown them toward the client. If they were down on the client, that was his responsibility. His assumed constraints had limited the whole team. How could he open their minds?

Suddenly, he had an idea.

He rummaged through his briefcase and found the scissors he'd taken from Cayla. He passed out a business card to each team member and said, "What if I asked you to cut a hole from my business card large enough to stick my head through?"

They stared at him.

"A hole is a space surrounded by continuous paper," he elaborated. "The paper must be one piece—no cutting it in two and joining ends around my head."

After giving his words a few seconds to sink in, he challenged them. "What are you thinking right now? What's going through your head about what I've just asked you to do? Jude, you're in production, what do you think? Maril? Alexa? Peter?"

Peter spoke first. "My first thought is, 'What's this got to do with anything?'"

Jude stated with conviction, "I don't think it can be done."

Maril said, "It can probably be done or you wouldn't be asking, but I certainly don't have the time to waste trying to figure it out right now."

Alexa jumped up, grabbed the scissors and a card, and started cutting concentric circles that fell out in a spiral. She seemed confident of her solution until she realized that she would have to cut the paper spiral to unravel it, and that would break the rules. In defeat she uttered, "I hate these puzzles. I can never figure them out."

After everyone else had responded, Peter reached for the scissors and a card. Quietly, he folded the card in half lengthwise. He cut a series of narrow slits from the folded edge to within a hairs-breadth of the opposite side.

Next he turned the card completely around so that the open edges were facing him. Going the opposite direction, he cut more slits between the other slits, again stopping within a hairs-breadth of the opposite end of the card.

Finally, he slipped the scissors into the fold and cut carefully. The group watched in awe as Peter unfolded the card. He pulled the slits apart as wide as they would go, revealing a fragile paper ring. Carefully, he slipped the ring over Steve's head and around his neck.*

The team broke into applause.

"I'm an art director," Peter explained, "and a lover of origami—the ancient Japanese art of paper folding. I've done stuff like this since I was a kid."

Maril looked at Steve. "This has been very entertaining and all, but what's the point?"

Steve sat down, clasped his hands in front of him on the table, and said, "Elephant thinking."

"Okay, I'll bite," Peter said.

---

* For instructions on how to perform this trick, see the Appendix.

Steve told them Cayla's elephant story. "Four of us had elephant thinking when challenged to cut the card. 'It can't be done, I don't have time, I'm not good at these kinds of things.' Our assumed constraints limited our belief that the trick could be done. But it turns out that one of us did have an answer."

"Assumed constraint," said Alexa, repeating the phrase. "What's that?"

"It's a belief that limits your experience," Steve said. "I now realize I gave up on the creative process because I assumed you and Peter should have all the answers. I gave up on Rhonda because I assumed she had given up on me. And I gave up on United Bank because I assumed they were nuts!" There. He'd spoken the truth.

Alexa let out a chuckle. "I'm not sure it's an assumed constraint to think the client is nuts. Maybe they are."

Steve felt uncomfortable when the team laughed at the client's expense. When the snickering died down he said, "I'm not sure I've been fair to United Bank. I'd like to suggest we all give them the benefit of the doubt. They've suffered because I haven't handled the situation well. If we lose them, the entire agency will suffer."

Jude looked at him with concern. "Do you really think we'll lose the account?" she asked.

"I don't know. When I tell Rhonda about their reaction to the presentation, my bet is we'll either lose me or the client."

"I've heard rumors that, uh, Grant was going to take over the account," Maril said haltingly. "How do you feel about that?"

Too stunned to answer, Steve sat for what felt like an eternity. He hadn't heard any rumors. He loathed the idea that people were talking about replacing him.

"How do you think I'd feel?" he finally mustered.

"Honestly? You've been so discouraged and frustrated that I thought maybe you'd be relieved," said Maril.

Steve felt completely exposed. He was transparent—not just to Cayla, but to his coworkers as well. How did he feel? He tended to be a thinker, not a feeler. Cayla's words flashed in his memory:

The greater gift is to know your own *mind.*

"I can see why you think I'd be relieved," Steve heard himself reply, "but I don't want to give up. I want to meet the challenge. I'm not sure where to start, except to ask for your forgiveness as I try to stop the ship from sinking."

"Steve," said Peter, "you know I don't care much for account executives—the best way to kill a creative idea is to run it through one of you guys."

Steve laughed, though he knew Peter was only half-kidding.

"But for the creative process to work," Peter continued, "artists need guidance and direction. That needs to come from you."

"Peter is right," Alexa said. "And the place to start is with the client. You've got to steer them in the right direction—even if they are difficult."

"You're right, of course," Steve said. "That's where I'll start. I'll get the budget issue ironed out and let you know what we decide."

The last fifteen minutes of the meeting were filled with enthusiastic energy as the team mapped out a plan. As they left the meeting room, each team member wished Steve luck.

I'll need it, he thought. What could he possibly say to the client to turn this thing around? And what about leading his team? He had challenged his assumed constraints with them, but now what? Would he be able to provide the direction they needed?

4

Cycles of Power

Steve was up early the next morning, even though it was a Saturday. The pressure he felt wouldn't let him sleep. He knew he needed an escape, even if for only a few hours. With dawn breaking, he went to the garage and pulled the cover off the majestic motorcycle that was his pride and joy. He rolled the gleaming Harley out to the street, strapped on his helmet, and threw his leg over the saddle. He started the motor and reveled in the powerful sound. He would spend this day as a wheeled warrior.

He shifted into gear and headed off. Thundering along the road, he realized there were so many things he loved about motorcycling—the proverbial wind in his face was only a small part of it. As he contemplated the joys of riding, he felt a sense of mastery over what he realized was actually a pretty inept machine. After all, a motorcycle couldn't even stand up by itself. Steve loved the synergy of riding—the melding of human and machine that gave capabilities and power to both that neither possessed separately.

The magic of the moment was interrupted when the bike started sputtering and slowing down. He pulled over to take a look. He had been off the bike for no more than a few minutes when he heard another cycle pull up. There's an unwritten code among bikers, so Steve knew it must be another biker stopping to see if he could be of service.

"Need any help?" The voice sounded familiar. He looked up from the wiring he'd been fiddling with and his jaw dropped open.

"Cayla?" he said, flabbergasted.

Cayla looked as surprised as Steve. "Wow, isn't this a coincidence?"

"Somehow I don't think so," Steve said.

"You know, when I met you at the café I thought you looked familiar, and now I think I know why. Are you a H.O.G.?" Cayla asked.

"Yeah, I am. But I haven't been to a Harley Owner Group meeting for months," Steve said.

"So how'd it go with your team yesterday?"

Steve gave her a noncommittal shrug.

"I'm guessing," Cayla continued, "but tell me if I'm wrong: Yesterday you accepted responsibility, challenged assumed constraints, and decided to fight for your job and the client. The problem is, you don't know where to begin. You feel powerless."

"There you go again, reading my mind!" Steve shook his head, not knowing what to believe. "But you're right. That's why I took time out for a ride."

Cayla looked at Steve's cycle. "What happened?" she asked.

"She died on me," he said. He tested the ignition but nothing happened. "I know I've got plenty of gas, so it's probably a bad battery or a fouled spark plug." He rummaged through his saddlebag, searching for a spare set of plugs.

"Let me help," Cayla said as she pulled a spare set from underneath her seat.

"Are you sure these aren't trick plugs?" Steve asked, only half-kidding.

Cayla seemed not to hear his comment. "It's a shame that help like this isn't more common in the real world, isn't it?"

Steve wasn't sure if Cayla was speaking of the real world outside of cycling enthusiasts, or the real world outside the strange one created every time he met her.

Cayla continued, "Listen, there's a dealer close by. Why don't you follow me over there, where you can replace the plugs I loaned you?"

"I didn't know there was a shop around here," Steve said.

"Yeah, Hal's Harleys—I've been going there for years."

"Hal's?" Steve recognized the name. "Hal's is legendary. I didn't know it was around here. Sounds like a good plan to me."

They fired up their engines and Cayla took the lead. Soon Steve was again immersed in the pure joy of riding, wondering why it gave him such a thrill. He was so engrossed in his own thoughts that he almost missed Cayla's signal as she took a left off the road. A few yards farther down they turned left again into the Harley-Davidson dealership. Before Steve could dismount, Cayla was standing beside him, helmet and glasses already off.

"Power." Cayla spoke the word in a resonant voice that evoked its meaning.

Steve was confused. "Excuse me?"

"Power," Cayla repeated. "It's why you love to ride."

Steve started to freak. "How did you know I was thinking about—"

"I'm a keen observer, remember? I've seen that look before—I've *had* that look before—where you are lost in the joy of riding and you're not quite sure why. Well, I know why. It's the power, the knife-edged control, and the independence that riding offers."

"I'm not sure I agree it's about power and control," Steve countered. "Riding is fun—pure and simple."

"When did you start riding?" Cayla asked.

Steve enjoyed reliving the story of his love affair with motorcycles. He told her about riding on the back of his dad's motorcycle, hardly able to wait until he was old enough to ride for himself. When he was thirteen, he'd talked his dad into buying him a small scooter. At sixteen, he'd made his first road trip, riding from Denver to the Nebraska state line with his younger brother.

"I loved the feeling of independence and freedom from all the rules and regulations I lived with in school," he said. "But I wasn't on a power trip."

"Maybe you should reconsider the way you define power," Cayla suggested gently.

Words began to flow through Steve's head: *abuse, corruption, coercion, control, authority, manipulation, money, domination.*

Cayla studied him closely. "Interesting," she said. "I imagine that most of the words you're thinking about are negative, because you've seen power misused so much."

Steve opened his mouth to comment, but Cayla threw out another question.

"Have you ever known someone who was in a powerful position, but you had no respect for them?" she asked.

Silly question, thought Steve, *of course I have*. In addition to a couple of executive types at work, he could add a number of politicians—as well as Roger from United Bank.

Cayla nodded as though agreeing with his unspoken thoughts. "Lord Acton wrote, 'Power tends to corrupt, and absolute power corrupts absolutely.' Steve, think about all the negative stereotypes we have about power today—it's a wonder anyone would ever want to be powerful."

"I guess you're right," Steve admitted. "But I'm not sure where you're going with this discussion."

"I think you're trying to avoid power and I'm trying to help you embrace it. In a way, you already do."

"Me, embrace power? Like when?"

"When you ride your bike. What you love about riding is the sense of power—the power of being one with the bike; the power that brings you a sense of control. When you ride, you feel free. Compare this feeling to the way you feel about your work right now."

Steve groaned. He was trying *not* to think about work for a couple of hours. And he sure didn't want to compare riding to work.

"Do you feel powerful at work?" Cayla challenged.

Being an account executive on United Bank should have made him feel empowered and free to do great work. Instead he felt restricted—stifled by others' expectations of him, burdened by his lack of experience with creative types, confused by a difficult client, and threatened by people such as Rhonda who were in positions that allowed them to determine his fate. Right now he certainly didn't have the feeling of being one with his job.

"In fact, I feel powerless," he confessed.

"Why do you think you feel that way?" Cayla asked.

"Because I'm not in a position to get people to do what I want them to do," Steve replied emphatically.

"Isn't that interesting?" Cayla strapped her helmet on the back of her bike and said,

✳

*"Not realizing
your own power
could be
your greatest
assumed constraint."*

✳

As she led him into the shop, Cayla said, "I want to introduce you to some people I think you'll appreciate. They all have discovered there are a lot of ways to influence others and achieve their goals. We'll start with Woody—one of the best parts managers in the country. Knows most of the part numbers by heart. It's amazing. Just watch."

They walked up to the parts counter and Cayla was greeted warmly by a gracious young man.

"Hey, Cayla! What can we do for you? The world treating you okay?" He extended a hand and smiled brightly.

Cayla gave him a hearty handshake. "Yeah! Or at least it *will* if you'll get my friend here a set of standard spark plugs. And can you ask one of the boys to check his electrical system? The beast died a few miles from here, and I had to rescue him." Cayla gave Steve a "just-teasing" jab in the arm.

The young man nodded at Steve. "Bike's not dead, right? Just resting." He smiled back at Cayla, cupped his hands together, and yelled, "Joey, pull me a set of 32310–78As."

Steve did a double take. The young man hadn't even looked up the part number.

Cayla smiled mischievously and turned back to the parts counter. "By the way, Woody, I'd like to introduce you to Steve. Steve, meet Woody, parts manager extraordinaire."

Woody pulled out an order form. "Glad to help you with the parts, but first let me give you my standard song and dance." At that, Woody stood at attention, cleared his throat, and in a rich baritone recited:

"*I stand behind the counter*
In a motorcycle store,
Sometimes I'm called a genius,
Sometimes I'm called much more.
Some questions are important;
Some questions aren't, but oh, my Lord,
I'm supposed to be an Edison
Combined with Henry Ford.
I claim I'm no mechanic
But when the job goes sick,
The mechanic comes and asks me
What makes the darn thing tick.
But life would be a pleasure
And I'd grin from ear to ear
If the customer'd only tell me
The model, make, and year."

Steve laughed and promptly gave Woody the requisite model, make, and year.

As he completed the order form, Woody called out to the parts man behind him, "I'll also need a 32591–80 and a set of 31986–65Cs. Thanks, Joey."

Steve was impressed. "That's quite a skill you have there. How did you memorize all those part numbers?"

"Oh, there's a method to the madness. Once you understand the underlying principles behind the numbering system, it's not that hard."

Woody pointed at Cayla. "Actually, she's the one who helped me realize that knowing the system and part numbers is an important *point of power*. It's really helped me build credibility in this industry. I've had a terrific career, and I don't even have a tattoo!"

Cayla cast a sideways glance at Woody and he laughed. "Okay, I do have one small tattoo. Can't get anything past her!"

"What do you mean, 'point of power'?" Steve asked.

"A lot of people think there's only one kind of power—position power—and if you don't have it, you're a puppet of those who do," Woody explained.

"I've heard that before," Steve said as he winked at Cayla. "That kind of thinking is very limiting, isn't it?"

"It sure is! The best way to explain that is to demonstrate how we activate points of power around here," Woody said. "Come on." He waved for them to come along as he led them to the service area.

Steve was enthralled by the hubbub of activity: mechanics joking, complaining, carrying on; cycles being rolled and towed and lifted; roaring engines being tested; customers questioning, concerned and nervous about the prognosis.

Woody explained, "When people bring their bikes in here, it's not as though they're bringing their motorcycles to a service department. It's more like they're bringing a child to the emergency ward. Our wrenches—mechanics, as lay people call 'em—obviously have **knowledge power**. They are experts at fixing Harleys. But they've also got **personal power**—their ability to give assurance to people and make them feel comfortable with the work that needs to be done and the costs involved. Cayla helped everyone understand that their personal power enhances their knowledge power. That combination has made us incredibly successful."

With that comment, one of the sweaty and soiled mechanics called over from his workbench:

"Before Cayla worked with us, no one thought mechanics had much personality, let alone personal power! But look at us," the mechanic said with a smile. "We're actually quite charming."

Everyone laughed. Steve admired their easy camaraderie.

"Come on," Cayla said, "Let's go meet Jim, head of sales. He has some interesting ideas about **relationship power**."

They found Jim in the showroom. As soon as Jim saw them, he walked over and gave Cayla a hug.

"Checking up on us, huh? Let me show you something!" Jim pulled a rumpled piece of paper out of his shirt pocket and proudly pointed to a list of numbers. "Look at these results from our latest customer sales and service report."

Cayla took the report from Jim and held it so that Steve could read along. "This is an incredible improvement over last time," Cayla noted. "What changed?"

"I've been in sales all my life, so I knew that relationships were vital. But somehow I got caught up in product information—I mean, it's easy to do when you love the product you're selling. I finally realized that I am good in sales because of my personal power—my people skills. People are my passion and I've built an incredible network. When I started to focus on those relationships, my sales and customer satisfaction increased. Sure, we sell and service Harley-Davidsons, but we're really in the people business."

"What exactly do you mean, 'focus on relationships'?" Steve asked.

"I began to see I had relationship power through my wonderful contacts—customers who were already happy with me and the dealership. I started cultivating those relationships and asking for leads. One relationship led to another. Now my problem is that I have all these great relationships and people who want to buy, and I have no motorcycles left! We've already sold out our annual allocation!"

"That's a nice problem to have," said Steve. "Let me ask you more about relationship power. I see how it works in sales, but how does it work in other parts of the shop?"

Jim discreetly pointed to a young woman working in the merchandise section of the showroom. "See the young woman by the leather jackets? That's Lisa, our apparel and accessories buyer. She's the daughter of the owner of the dealership. That's relationship power."

Steve frowned. "I'm not sure most people find nepotism a positive use of power."

"Ah," Jim said thoughtfully. "That's where most of us go wrong. We don't acknowledge our power because we're afraid of what others might think. But having power means you have a choice to use it—or not. It certainly doesn't mean you have to abuse it.

"When we first started discussing the issue of power here at the shop, Cayla asked each of us to write down what we thought our points of power were. Lisa didn't have 'Dad' down on her list. We all told her she should. She protested. She said she wanted to succeed on her own merit, not just because she's the owner's daughter. She was very sensitive about it.

"You know what I told her? 'Fool! If my dad were the owner of the shop, I'd take advantage of it. You can talk to him and get information that the rest of us can't. If you use your relationship power to do a better job and help the shop, then that's using your power in a positive way and we'll all be grateful, not jealous or resentful.' "

"Lisa got the job because it's her dad's business," Cayla added, "but she keeps it because of her knowledge and personal power."

Steve nodded. It was something he'd have to think about.

"You don't have to agree with everything, Steve, just take it into account," said Cayla.

Woody grabbed Steve's arm and led him down the hall. "Speaking of accounts, let me introduce you to Dee Dee, our bookkeeper."

Approaching the bookkeeper's desk, Steve said, "Nice to meet you, Dee Dee. In what way are you powerful?"

Dee Dee either didn't notice or chose to ignore the hint of irony in Steve's voice. "I have **task power**," she said confidently. "I used to think I was low person on the totem pole around here. I mean, my job is the only one that doesn't deal directly with motorcycles. But I was wrong about that."

Jim jumped in. "Dee Dee really runs this joint. She's the one who cuts paychecks, withholds taxes, pays expenses, invoices our customers, and manages our bank accounts. Hard to believe she didn't see herself as having any power!"

"I used to think power was held only by people like our owner—people who have **position power**," said Dee Dee.

"So did I," said Steve, "but now I understand there are many forms of power."

"Acknowledging the power you have gives you a sense of control over your job and your choices," said Dee Dee. "I appreciate my work much more now, even though I don't have position power."

"Are you implying there's no need for position power?" asked Steve.

"I hope not!"

At the sound of the voice, they all turned around. Standing behind them was a well-built man with a gray ponytail down his back. The man extended his hand to Steve.

"Nice to meet you. I'm Hal, the owner of this shop, and I'm here to tell you that position power is a good thing to have. But I've learned a great lesson: The best leadership situation is where you have position power and never have to use it! Like money in the bank, even though you never need it, it's nice to know it's there. Besides, it's better to have people work with you—not for you."

Hal pointed to a plaque on the counter. "This is our leadership credo," he said.

THERE'S ONLY POWER
IN EMPOWERMENT
IF YOU ARE A SELF LEADER.

"That credo must work," Steve said. "Hal's Harley is legendary and now I know why—you have all kinds of self leaders around here."

"They sure do," said Cayla, "and one of the ways they have become effective self leaders is by understanding the five kinds of power." With that, she pointed to a poster on the wall:

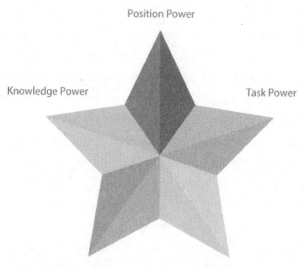

Position Power

Knowledge Power

Task Power

Relationship Power

Personal Power

POINTS OF POWER

"As you can see," Cayla continued, "the first point of power is **knowledge power** as Woody has; second is **personal power** as the service reps have; third is **relationship power** as Jim and Lisa have; fourth is **task power** as Dee Dee has; and fifth is **position power** as Hal has."

Steve furrowed his brow. "I think I get it now," he said. "You need to know the nature of your strengths—your power—before you can lead yourself."

"That's right!" Cayla said. "How can you lead yourself if you don't realize that you *have* sources of power? Everyone has different types of power in their lives and work." Cayla paused a moment to let that sink in. "Each point of power can contribute to your success—or become the weak link. When I found you on the side of the road, it was a simple little spark plug that had disabled a powerful, complex machine.

"The message is: Identify and recognize your points of power and cultivate them. But it is important to remember what the philosopher Balthazar Gracián wrote, 'The sole advantage of power is that you can do more good.' "

"That's the first time I've ever heard power discussed as a tool for doing good," Steve confessed.

Cayla nodded knowingly. "How can you do more good for yourself, your family, your team, your organization, or your community if you don't have power?"

"I see your point," said Steve.

As they headed to the exit, Steve realized he'd been to dozens of motorcycle shops, but had never enjoyed hanging around one as much as he had this day. It wasn't just the hardware, noise, activity, and smells he loved. He realized it was the people he really enjoyed. These were enthusiasts, folks who loved what they did every day. They were people who had a sense of their unique points of power.

As he passed the parts counter, Steve waved good-bye to Woody.

"Don't forget your parts!" Woody said, pointing to a brown paper bag sitting on the counter.

"Oh yeah, thanks. And speaking of thanks, where'd Cayla go?" Steve asked as he looked around the showroom.

Woody glanced around and shrugged his shoulders. "Don't know," he said as he put the receipt in Steve's bag. "Hey, it was great to meet you! Ride safe!"

Outside the shop, Cayla's motorcycle was gone. Steve reached into his bag for the replacement parts and pulled out what he thought was the receipt. But instead it was a paper slip with a printed message:

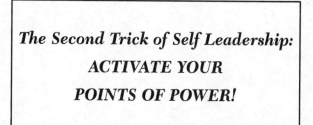

The Second Trick of Self Leadership:
ACTIVATE YOUR
POINTS OF POWER!

Steve shook his head in wonder. Was there no end to Cayla's tricks?

He fired up his big V-twin and notched it into first gear. As he roared away, he could hear Cayla's voice in his mind:

Perhaps your greatest assumed constraint is not realizing your own power.

He would think about that later, when he figured out what to do about his job. For the moment he didn't want to think—he just wanted to ride—no, he *needed* to ride. It made him feel powerful.

5

Diagnose Yourself

Bright and early Monday morning, Steve headed for Cayla's Café, determined to save his job and keep his client. If Cayla couldn't help him, maybe the caffeine would. He'd spent Sunday poring over his files, notes, and proposals, looking for the flaw that had caused the client to reject the plan. In the process he realized that the only point of power he had with United Bank was task power. To restore the client's confidence, he would need knowledge power—and for that, he needed help.

Steve entered the café, keeping an eye out for Cayla. He made his way to the counter and just as he was about to ask the barista if Cayla was in, Steve heard the whistling. He turned around and sure enough, she was sitting at their regular table, as though waiting for him. Steve smiled and went over to join her.

"Where did you disappear to on Saturday?" Steve asked. "I still had questions."

"I thought you needed to be alone to process all you learned at Hal's," Cayla explained. "Where is your thinking now?"

"I've analyzed everything to death. I just can't figure out what's wrong with the budget and strategy I already proposed," Steve said with a sigh.

"Have you ever worked with a client to develop a comprehensive ad campaign before?" Cayla asked.

"No, but I've drawn up dozens of budgets over the years, and the strategy depends on the budget."

Cayla pulled out two rubber bands and wove them together. "I'm going to use a magic trick as a metaphor for your situation. Will you play along with me?"

Steve shrugged his shoulders. "Sure. Is this that cool trick you showed the kids the day we met?"

Cayla nodded. "An old Indian mystic taught me the art of mind over matter," she began. Cayla the mentor transformed before Steve's eyes into Cayla the magician. As she separated the tangled bands from each other, it appeared she was moving matter through matter.

Having seen the trick before, Steve tried to detect the illusion. But Cayla's performance was flawless. He found himself as delighted as the children had been—not because it was magic, but because he appreciated her skill.

"Amazing!" he said.

"Thank you," said Cayla. "Your goal, Steve, is to astound someone with this magic trick by this time next week."

Steve laughed. He would enjoy sharing the trick with his girlfriend, Blair. He still hadn't told her what was going on at work. He knew Blair sensed something was wrong, but over the years she had learned to give him his space until he was ready to talk. It would be fun to lighten things up for her. "Okay, where do I start?"

"By asking yourself two questions about the goal of performing the magic trick: First, what is your level of competence? Second, what is your level of commitment? Let's start with the first question—your competence."

"I'm definitely competent!" Steve said confidently. "I watched you very carefully and saw exactly what you did, so I'm pretty sure I can do it."

"Okay, let's see how competent you are." Cayla handed him the rubber bands.

Steve took the two bands and entangled them the way he remembered Cayla doing. He flexed and stretched the bands, attempting to separate them. The bands shot off his fingers and flew across the shop. Embarrassed, he stood to fetch them, but Cayla held her arm out and stopped him.

"I thought this might happen," she said as she pulled a large bag of rubber bands out of her case.

"What did I do wrong?" Steve asked.

"You acted as though you had competence when, in fact, you didn't," Cayla replied.

"That's harsh," Steve accused.

"No, it's simply the truth, and you needn't be ashamed. Competence means you have the knowledge and skill to accomplish the goal or do the skill in question. If you've never done the trick before, then you can't possibly have knowledge or skill. You are at the learning stage. What's wrong with that? You can't expect to be competent on a trick you've never done and have no idea how to do."

"I guess you're right. Okay, show me how."

Cayla took two rubber bands and placed them strategically on the thumb and index finger of each hand. She performed the trick slowly and deliberately.

Steve shook his head in admiration. "I think I get it now, but I suppose I'll have to practice before I'm actually competent. By the way, you said I was supposed to ask myself two questions about the goal. The first question was about my level of competence, but I forget the second one. What was it again?"

"The second question is, what is your level of commitment? Commitment is measured by your motivation and confidence about the goal," Cayla explained.

"When we started I was motivated and confident. Now I'm not so sure! I thought the trick would be easier than it's turning out to be."

"That's exactly what happens as you move through the Development Continuum!" Cayla said enthusiastically.

"The what? Are you taking me into a magical space-time continuum thing?" Steve joked.

"The Development Continuum is simply a model of four stages people usually experience when they are learning to master something." Cayla reached into her magic case and pulled out a glossy card, which she handed to Steve.

Development Levels

"In terms of the rubber band trick, look at these four stages and tell me which one you think you started in and where you are now." Cayla's eyes were bright, as though she were about to reveal a great secret.

Steve studied the graphic and pointed to the square on the right. "I guess I started here, at D1, with low competence but high commitment. Now I feel like I'm at D2—low competence with low commitment."

"That's normal," she said. "When you first begin to learn something or take on a goal, you have this naïve enthusiasm that overshadows your lack of competence. Once you get into the goal and realize you don't have the competence, your expectations are shattered."

"Reality shock," Steve said, nodding his head knowingly.

"Exactly!" Cayla seemed pleased with Steve's understanding. "D2, which is short for Development Level 2, is a natural stage of learning. It's where you realize there is a discrepancy between the expectations you had in the beginning—Development Level 1 or D1—and the reality of the current situation."

"So, everyone goes through this reality shock every time they are learning to do something?" Steve asked.

"The Development Continuum captures what people typically experience, so you can be better prepared to handle what will probably happen. It helps you recognize how your competence and commitment change as you learn something new or pursue a goal. Significant research validates these stages of development, but if you simply think about the goals you've accomplished—and ones you haven't—you'll realize your own experience is proof enough," Cayla said.

Steve picked up two more rubber bands as he reflected on Cayla's words. He entwined the bands, making sure they were placed on his fingers and thumbs the way he'd seen Cayla do it. He stretched and twisted them for show, then attempted to do the sleight-of-hand that would separate them as if by magic. Again, one of the bands went flying—almost hitting Cayla in the forehead.

Steve would have laughed if he hadn't been so mortified that he'd nearly poked out Cayla's eye.

"Okay. Stop, right there." Cayla held up both hands. "How do you feel about the trick now?"

"Frustrated, discouraged, disappointed," Steve said.

"That's why the second development level, D2, is called the disillusioned learner stage."

"What are the other stages called?" Steve asked.

"The first development level, D1, is called the **enthusiastic beginner** stage. That's where you began. If you make it through the second level, the D2 or **disillusioned learner** stage—where you are now—then you reach D3, which is known as the **capable but cautious performer** stage. Finally, when you have mastered the skill, you reach D4 or the **self-reliant achiever** stage."

"Excuse me, Cayla, but you said *if* I make it through the second stage of the disillusioned learner, then I go to the third stage of capable but cautious performer. What happens if I don't make it?"

"You tell me," Cayla said.

Steve reflected a moment. "That's where I give up and quit, right?"

"Right," Cayla confirmed. "So, that's your dilemma on the magic trick right now, is it not? You realize it is going to take practice to master it, and you're not sure it's worth it. Am I right?"

"As usual."

"So quit."

"I just might." Steve sounded like a little boy defying his mother.

"It's always your choice to quit or keep going," Cayla reminded him. "But sometimes you give up without conscious choice, so it feels like failure."

"Are you suggesting that if I choose to quit, then it's not failure?"

"When you are at the disillusioned learner stage of your goal and you lack competence and commitment, you are not a failure if you *thoughtfully* decide it is not worth the time and effort to proceed," she said. "You are a self leader proactively accepting responsibility."

"What if I don't want to quit?" Steve asked.

"I'll answer that question next time. That's the end of your lesson for today," she said with finality.

Steve couldn't hide his disappointment. "My lesson? What is my lesson? I've learned that I'm at the second stage of disillusioned learner on the magic trick and I'm about ready to quit my job—and that's my lesson?"

"Your lesson is to think about what it will take for you to get to the next level of development," Cayla announced as she headed toward her office.

Steve followed, feeling a sense of déjà vu at the now familiar scene of Cayla rifling through files and drawers to find what she wanted.

"Here it is." She handed Steve a crumpled sheet.

When I am at D1, the **enthusiastic beginner** level of development, with low competence and high commitment, I need:

_____

_____

When I am at D2, the **disillusioned learner** level of development, with low to some competence and low commitment, I need:

_____

_____

When I am at D3, the **capable but cautious** level of development, with moderate to high competence and variable commitment, I need:

_____

_____

When I am at D4, the **self-reliant achiever** level of development, with high competence and high commitment, I need:

_____

_____

"Your homework assignment is to write down what you would need to help you progress from enthusiastic beginner to self-reliant achiever on this rubber band trick," Cayla said. "Remember, I want you to amaze your family and friends with it by this time next week."

"What do you mean, what I would need?"

Cayla stopped dead in her tracks. "Excellent question." She slapped her open hand to her forehead, "I can't believe I forgot!" She took the sheet from his hand and turned it over to reveal two columns on the back.

Steve was puzzled. He could have sworn the back of the sheet was blank when she first handed it to him.

Pointing to the two columns, she said, "These are examples of what you need to increase your competence and build commitment if you are going to progress from enthusiastic beginner to self-reliant achiever on a goal."

Steve turned the sheet over before focusing on the back side, still wondering how he could have missed noticing the two columns.

COMPETENCE

To increase your competence to achieve a goal, you need:

DIRECTION

from someone who will:

1. Set a clear goal
2. Generate an action plan
3. Show you how to do the goal or skill
4. Clarify roles
5. Provide timelines
6. Establish priorities
7. Monitor and evaluate your work and give feedback

COMMITMENT

To build your commitment to achieve a goal, you need:

SUPPORT

from someone who will:

1. Listen to you
2. Recognize and appreciate your efforts
3. Facilitate your problem solving
4. Ask you for input
5. Provide rationale (remind you why you're doing it)
6. Share information about their experiences relevant to the goal
7. Share information about the organization relevant to the goal

"I hope this helps clarify what I meant," Cayla said. "When your competence is low, you need direction; when your commitment is low, you need support."

"What's the difference between direction and support?"

"Good question," said Cayla. "Directive behavior is hands-on. It involves deciding, teaching, observing, and providing frequent feedback. Supportive behavior is more about listening, involving, facilitating, and encouraging. If you can learn to diagnose your own development level on any given task, you'll know what you need to ask for to succeed."

"Fine, but once I know what to ask for—who do I ask?"

"That depends," Cayla said. "If it's about the magic trick, you can obviously ask me, other magicians, or even research online. What if it's about your United Bank ad campaign? Who do you ask for help on that?"

"Excellent question," Steve said. He felt as though he'd been jolted back into reality. He'd been so wrapped up in the magic trick and learning about the Development Continuum, he'd forgotten that the real point of it all was to save his job.

"Think of your goal for the United Bank account," Cayla said. "Think about the skills required to be an account executive and orchestrate their ad campaign. Then diagnose your development level on each skill. Remember,

✲

*When your **competence**
is low, you need
direction;
when your
commitment
is low, you need
support.*"

✲

"I think I've got it!" Steve gave Cayla a high five and gathered his papers. He was eager to complete his homework and see how his new knowledge applied to his job.

6

Getting What You Need

It wasn't until later the next day that Steve finally had time to focus on Cayla's homework. He wrote out the answers to the questions, using the Competence and Commitment lists as a guide.

- *When I am at* **D1**—*the* **enthusiastic beginner** *level of development with low competence and high commitment*—*I need:*
  High direction and low support

- *When I am at* **D2**—*the* **disillusioned learner** *level of development with low to some competence and low commitment*—*I need:*
  High direction and high support

- When I am at **D3**—*the* **capable but cautious** *level of development with moderate to high competence and variable commitment—I need:*
  Low direction and high support

- When I am at **D4**—*the* **self-reliant achiever** *level of development with high competence and high commitment—I need:*
  Low direction and low support

Steve confirmed that he was at the disillusioned learner stage with the rubber band trick—he knew more than when he started, but still couldn't perform the trick and wasn't sure he ever would.

Now Steve was ready to apply the development levels to his own job. He began by listing what he had been responsible for when he was Rhonda's assistant: production budgets, media budgets, and production schedules. He diagnosed that his development level was the same in all of those areas, and that his needs were also the same on each:

Goal: prepare and deliver production budgets, media budgets, and production schedules for Rhonda's accounts within expected timelines.
My Development Level: D4—self-reliant achiever
I Needed: low direction and low support

In the past he would discuss accounts with Rhonda and propose budgets for production or media. He had also taken her input and created production schedules. "Piece of cake—I was at D4 on all the above," he said aloud. But that was then. Now he didn't even have the confidence to do the things he used to take for granted. He made a note: *Used to be a D4—but I think I've gone backward!*

He turned his attention to what was happening now and asked himself, *What goals and tasks am I responsible for as an account executive for the United Bank account?* It was then that he had his aha moment. His role with United Bank now was very different from what his role had been when he worked with Rhonda—yet he'd considered them the same. There was a big difference between preparing a budget based on Rhonda's input and having to develop one from scratch. He didn't have any idea where to begin—let alone how to sell United Bank on it. Considering the current circumstances, he acknowledged his new goal:

> **Goal:** get buy-in from United Bank for production budget, media budget, and production schedule
> **My Development Level:** D2—disillusioned learner
> **I Need:** high direction and high support

As he continued, Steve began to see a pattern:

Goal: provide creative team with positioning and content statements
My Development Level: D2—disillusioned learner
I Need: high direction and high support

Goal: provide media buyer with demographic targets, budget, and buying strategy
My Development Level: D2—disillusioned learner
I Need: high direction and high support

Steve shook his head in dismay—no wonder he was about to lose the account. He needed high direction and high support and he had gotten neither. He wondered if this was the third trick of self leadership.

Suddenly the phone rang and jolted him into the present. It was Marsha from accounting, reminding him that they needed his expense forms before the end of the day. "No problem," Steve said, even though it was.

Steve pulled out his expense file. This is one area where he knew he was at D3—the capable but cautious performer stage. He had high competence to complete the expense forms, but his commitment was variable. He was confident he could complete the forms; he just had no motivation to do so.

Need: *low direction and high support*

He looked back at Cayla's list to see which of the supportive behaviors might stop him from procrastinating. Was there someone or some way to keep him from turning in forms at the last minute? What could he do to overcome his belief that this was nothing more than bureaucratic busywork? Again, questions for Cayla.

Steve finally completed the paperwork and dropped it off to accounting, hoping no one would notice it was late. It was long past 5:00 p.m., but he had one last bit of business: to clear his voicemail.

"You have one new message," the familiar recording announced. Steve pressed "3" to listen.

"Steve, this is Rhonda. We need to talk. I just picked up a message from Roger at United Bank and he is not pleased. I understand your presentation didn't go over well. It would have been nice to hear it from you instead of the client. This sounds serious. Meet me at Irma's Eatery for lunch at noon next Monday. I told Roger I'd handle it, but you need to bring me up to speed. Bring me a copy of the original proposal. See you Monday."

Steve hung up and sat down. He had hoped for more time to put a comprehensive plan together. Now he had just four business days. At least he'd made progress. He'd accepted responsibility for what happened at United Bank. He'd broken through his assumed constraints that the fault was with the client and creative team. He had acknowledged his task power and his need for more knowledge power. He had diagnosed himself at D2—the disillusioned learner stage—with low to some competence and low commitment on major aspects of the project. He knew he needed high direction and high support. Finally, he knew there were areas of the project where he used to be at D4—the self-reliant achiever stage—but now he realized he wasn't sure about his commitment.

What he hadn't done was figure out what to say to Rhonda and how to save the account. Now he had only until noon next Monday to decide if he would hand in his resignation or fight to keep his job. He thought he was through blaming Rhonda, but he felt the anger rising again. She held his fate in her hands and he didn't know if he could trust her or not.

On Friday, Steve headed back to Cayla's Café, homework in hand. He found her sitting at their table reading a book. Barely glancing up, she asked, "How'd you do on your homework?"

"I was hoping the teacher would check my work." Steve used a lighthearted tone that he hoped would cover the tension he felt.

"What's wrong?" Cayla asked.

So much for hiding my emotions from Cayla, Steve thought. "My boss, Rhonda, left me a message. Roger from United Bank called her, none too happy. She's meeting me on Monday to 'discuss the account.'" Steve drew quotes in the air to emphasize the last three words.

"Sounds as though we'd better speed up your learning cycle," Cayla said as she cleared the table. "Do you have the card I gave you that shows the Development Continuum?"

Steve found the dog-eared card in his notebook and handed it to Cayla.

Cayla tore the card in half.

"What are you doing?" Steve said, trying to keep his voice down.

Cayla stacked the two halves together and tore them in two.

"Oh, a trick?" Steve allowed.

Cayla took the four pieces and put them in the palm of her left hand. She laid her right palm on top, encasing the torn shards of paper between her two palms. She then raised her hands in prayer position and rubbed her palms back and forth as though grinding the pieces together.

"If this comes out in one piece, I'm going to freak," Steve said, more to himself than to Cayla.

Situational Leadership® II Model

Sure enough, when Cayla opened her hands, one piece of paper fell to the table. Her eyes met Steve's, then she looked back down at the piece of paper, beckoning him to pick it up. Steve tentatively took the paper, unfolded it, and puzzled over the new image.

"What do the different colors mean?" asked Steve.

"It's color-coded. For each development level, there is a corresponding leadership style to provide you with the appropriate amount of direction and/or support you need. At the D1—enthusiastic beginner stage, you need an S1 leadership style: ***directing***. At the D2—disillusioned learner stage, you need an S2 leadership style: ***coaching***. At the D3—capable but cautious performer stage, you need an S3 leadership style: ***supporting***. At the D4—self-reliant achiever stage, you need an S4 leadership style: ***delegating***. Pull out your homework and let's compare your answers with the model."

"I think I deserve high marks for this," Steve said, giving himself a verbal pat on the back. "The SLII® Model will make it easy to remember, but I think I did a good job of figuring it out from the lists of directive and supportive behaviors you gave me to use as reference."

"Definitely an A plus," Cayla concurred after studying his work. "And you deserve special credit for understanding regression."

Steve was afraid he'd get marked down for not knowing what she meant, so he smiled as though he did. Cayla must have sensed this, because she proceeded to explain what she meant.

"You picked up on the idea that you can be at the D4—self-reliant achiever stage on something and regress backwards to the D3—capable but cautious stage," she said.

"*Regression* is a great word to describe what happened to me," Steve said. "I was at the self-reliant achiever stage on budgets and production scheduling when I worked with Rhonda. But I've become so discouraged lately that if she called me to do the same things I used to do, I'm not sure I'd have the confidence to do them. I've definitely regressed from the self-reliant achiever stage to the capable but cautious performer stage."

"Good diagnosis," Cayla said. "You also seem to understand that in your new role as an account executive, you began at the D1—enthusiastic beginner stage, gathering information from the client, analyzing their needs, and generating a plan from scratch. But now you are at the D2—disillusioned learner stage."

"It's embarrassing, but I was so naïve that I didn't know I was supposed to gather information from the client in the first place. I was enthusiastically trying to create plans from thin air! When it didn't work, I quickly moved to disillusionment."

"It's all a part of the learning process," Cayla said.

Steve sighed. "If I'd known about the development stages from the beginning, I could have worked with Rhonda to get my needs met. The question now is, is it too late?"

"It's never too late to try," Cayla said. "I'm sure you'll find some answers this weekend as you prepare for your lunch meeting with Rhonda."

At the mention of the weekend, Steve realized he was already late for his Friday-night dinner with Blair.

7

Running Together

Blair was waiting patiently when Steve arrived. He was relieved to see her, but feeling guilty. He should have texted to tell her he was running late.

"Sorry to keep you waiting," he said as he gave her a heartfelt hug.

"I was afraid something happened," she said.

Steve heard genuine concern—not scolding—in her voice.

"You've been so busy we haven't gotten together all week. What's going on?" she asked.

"A lot," Steve replied.

"You okay?"

"Physically, yes," he said cryptically.

Over dinner at their favorite Mexican restaurant, Steve shared the strange events of the past week. He began with the botched ad campaign proposal for United Bank and how it led to meeting Cayla.

"She taught me something," he said. He pulled out one of his business cards and asked Blair if she had a pair of scissors in her purse.

She pulled out a tiny pair of cuticle scissors. "Will these do?"

With a straight face, Steve asked her to cut a hole in the card large enough for him to put his head through.

"That's why you're upset? A strange woman asked you to cut a hole in your business card and stick your head through it?"

Steve laughed for the first time that evening, "Partly," he kidded. "Go ahead. Try it."

"It's a trick." Blair put the scissors down and crossed her arms, refusing to play.

"You're absolutely right! Actually, it's the first trick of a self leader." Steve told her about elephant thinking and the importance of challenging assumed constraints. He then took the scissors, cut the card into a large ring, and placed it over her head. The people at the next table—who'd been stealing glances their way—clapped in appreciation.

"Okay," Blair said, "so what did you do with this revelation about assumed constraints?"

Steve described the meeting with his team, where he'd realized that his assumptions about his team members, the client, and his role had made him a victim. "I'm not exactly a natural-born leader," he said with a shake of his head.

Blair reached out and touched his hand. "Is that why I didn't see you last weekend—because you're feeling down on yourself? Did your motorcycle ride help at all?"

"I almost forgot about that—and it's the strangest part yet."

"What happened?" Blair asked.

Steve told her about his Harley dying and his bizarre roadside meeting with Cayla. He described the trip to the legendary Hal's Harley dealership, the conversation about power, and the mysterious "receipt" revealing the second trick of self leadership.

"So what's the trick?" she asked, sounding both curious and skeptical.

Steve handed the receipt to her.

" 'Activate your points of power,' " Blair said, reading from the slip of paper.

"I certainly didn't use my points of power with the United Bank account project," Steve said. "I should have been the one initiating action and directing others."

"But how could you lead others when you didn't even know what you were doing? You've never been an account executive before." Blair's statement surprised Steve. How could it be so clear to her when he had needed Cayla to point it out to him?

"I finally realized that today. I think I'm in the midst of learning the final trick. At first I diagnosed myself at the D1 (enthusiastic beginner) stage on almost every aspect of my role, but because I didn't get the S1 (direction leadership) style I needed, I'm now at the D2 (disillusioned learner) stage, and I need an S2 (coaching leadership) style. On some things, such as budgeting and scheduling, I was at the D4 (self-reliant achiever) stage and fine with an S4 (delegating leadership) style. But now I'm not sure I'm as competent as I thought, so I've regressed to the D3 (capable but cautious performer) stage, requiring an S3 (supporting) style of leadership." The words tumbled from Steve without pause.

When he was finished, Blair was staring blankly at him. "I have no idea what you just said."

Steve roared with laughter. "I must sound like I'm speaking a foreign language. Wait—just a second." Steve rose from the table and disappeared around the corner. When he returned, he had two rubber bands that he'd managed to get from the restaurant's front desk.

"I was talking about the four stages of learning and mastering something new," he said. "I'm going to show you a rubber band trick as an example." He began teaching Blair the magic trick, pulling out the card with the SLII® and using it for reference.

Situational Leadership® II Model

After a few minutes, they decided they were both at D2 on the rubber band trick.

Blair's eyes grew bright as she saw the connection between the rubber band trick and Steve's work.

"So as far as your job goes, you've diagnosed yourself at the D2–disillusioned learner stage on most of your important goals, and you've determined that you need more direction and support to succeed in your job." Blair frowned. "So where do you go from here?"

Steve confided that he had until noon on Monday to figure it out. "I'm not sure if I should resign and end the pain or fight for my job and risk having Rhonda fire me. What do you think?"

"I think you are very lucky to have run into Cayla," Blair said. "I'll make you a deal. If you'll help me with my 10K run tomorrow, I'll help you think through a plan for your meeting with Rhonda."

"Oh, man! I've been so wrapped up in my own problems I forgot you have your first race tomorrow." Steve shook his head. "I want to help, but I'm not sure what I can do between now and tomorrow morning."

"Here's my diagnosis," Blair said, referring to the model. "When it comes to my training schedule, I'm capable of the short runs during the week. But I've never had the confidence to finish that 10K practice run on the weekend. I think I'm at the D3–capable but cautious performer stage. For the race tomorrow I'm at the D2–disillusioned learner stage. I've never run in a race with hundreds of people before, so my competence is low. I don't know how I'll react and I'm afraid. Guess that means my commitment is low. What if I can't finish?"

"Come on, Blair," Steve encouraged. "You can *walk* six miles if you have to."

"What if I come in last? I'll be horrified." Blair put her hands over her eyes as though trying to block out the image of her straggling across the finish line long after the others had completed the race.

Steve laughed. "You *are* a disillusioned learner! How can I support you?"

Blair's impish smile made Steve wonder what he'd gotten himself into.

"I have relationship power with you, and I'm going to use it. Here's my request: Run with me. You've run in dozens of races and know what it's like. You have knowledge power. Be my running partner and coach. I need an S2–coaching leadership style, with both direction and support."

"Are you kidding? I haven't trained," Steve complained.

"As slow as I am, you don't need training to keep up!"

Blair and Steve kept talking on their way back from dinner. As he was driving home, Steve realized that because he'd taught the model to Blair, they now had a common framework to discuss where they were on their goals and what they needed to reach them.

As the sun came up Saturday morning, Steve put on his running gear, did some quick warm-ups, and headed out the door to pick up Blair.

Blair beamed when she saw Steve in his running clothes. "I knew you'd go for it." She handed him a bagel and a sport drink. "I have a feeling you might need these."

"I couldn't turn down a self leader in need," Steve said with a smile. "You asked for help and that takes strength."

They got into the car and headed out for the race. After a few minutes of silence Blair said, "I was thinking about the two tricks Cayla taught you—to challenge assumed constraints and activate your points of power. Those are potent concepts. I wouldn't be a runner at all if I hadn't used them—I just wasn't aware I was using them."

"Explain," Steve urged.

"Remember when I first started running? I bought cute shorts and tops, running shoes, good socks. I had all the best stuff. I was feeling very proud of myself. I took off down the street, ran the first block, and began to feel my thigh muscles tighten. I tried to control my breathing, but I couldn't get any air. I got that side stitch that wouldn't go away."

Steve chuckled. "I remember your excuse. You said, 'I must have fast twitch muscles. They're not really built for long-distance running.' "

"That was my assumed constraint. Although I used to be a pretty good sprinter, I assumed I couldn't run long distances well. You helped me challenge that assumed constraint by explaining that running uses very different muscles than what I was used to. You told me it was going to require more effort than buying good shoes."

"I nailed that one," Steve said proudly.

"The point is, I wanted to quit. I started off at the D1–enthusiastic beginner stage and it only took me two blocks to get to the D2–disillusioned learner stage!"

"So what did you need?" Steve asked.

"To my credit, I realized I needed coaching, so I could learn to run differently. I needed someone to observe, monitor, and evaluate my running; someone to show me how by giving me feedback. I needed an S1–directing leadership style, but since I never got it, I was at the point where I needed an S2–coaching style of leadership."

"I remember now," said Steve. "You went to a friend who was a high school cross-country coach and he helped you put a training program together. You used your relationship power to find someone with knowledge power."

"That's right," said Blair. "My coach helped me map out an entire strategy that included a running support group, getting feedback on my breathing and running technique, subscribing to a running magazine, and recruiting you to encourage me to keep up with my training schedule."

"You went out and hired a coach and he helped you achieve your goal," said Steve.

"Which reminds me of a favorite quote," said Blair:

✹

*"A person who does not
have a goal
is used by
someone who does."*

✹

"That's true," Steve agreed. "And sometimes our goals aren't reached because we let assumed constraints defeat us."

"Or we don't use our points of power," added Blair. "It occurred to me that a big mistake we make in our jobs is thinking that the only place to get direction and support is from our managers. But as you realized with your team the other day, that's an assumed constraint. Steve, you have a number of people and resources you can tap to get the direction and support you need to turn this United Bank account around. I have a feeling you have points of power you haven't begun to activate."

"You're probably right." Steve slowed as he approached the turn that would take them to the starting point of the race.

"We need to map out a strategy for your meeting with Rhonda, just like I did with my running. I think it will work!"

"If it doesn't, I can always fall back on my exit strategy and quit," Steve said.

Blair sighed. "Threatening to quit is just your way of feeling some sense of control when you're faced with a tough goal."

"Maybe." Steve pulled into the parking lot where hundreds of runners were congregated. "What is your goal today?" he asked. "What time are you trying to make?"

"Forget time. My goal is just to complete the 10K."

"Fair enough. If just finishing the race is motivating to you, that's what we'll focus on doing. But I think you should set a standard," he said. Pointing to a woman who appeared to be in her eighties, he said, "I think you should try to beat her."

Blair didn't take the bait. "That's not a smart goal! I have no control over how fast that woman runs. It'd be just my luck that she holds the national title for senior women."

"Shouldn't you have *some* standard?" Steve asked.

"How about this: My goal is not to be the last one over the finish line. That means that if I can't continue, you have to carry me over!"

They made their way to the registration table, picked up their numbers, and pinned them on their T-shirts. All kinds of people milled around the booths that offered food, drink, products, promotions, and massages. Music filled the air. The atmosphere was electric and Steve felt energized. It was fun just being part of the event.

People were gathering at the starting line. Blair and Steve were positioned midway in the pack when Blair darted forward, weaving her way to the front. She turned back and signaled Steve to follow her.

She doesn't know the front of the pack is reserved for qualified runners and sponsored professionals! Steve thought. He wondered if she would notice that the numbers pinned to their shirts were in the range of 001–100 and hers was 2045. As she reached the front row, he realized she was too pumped up to notice much of anything.

"On your mark," the starter bellowed from the PA system. Steve hadn't reacted in time to stop Blair. "Get set." The shot of the starting gun rang out, and they were off.

The exhilaration he had at the start of a race thrilled Steve. He could feel the ground shaking from the thousands of feet pounding behind him. He heard the collective breathing of hundreds of runners. By the time he caught up with Blair, dozens of runners had passed them by.

"Unbelievable!" Blair shouted. "Why are people running so fast this early in the race? I'll never finish if I try to keep up. I'm already ready to give up! What should I do, coach?"

"Pace yourself. Just make it to the fountain."

"Okay, so I make it to the fountain, then what?" she asked, breathing hard.

"Feel the spray coming off the fountain. It's invigorating! And, remember your goal."

"Oh, yeah. Finish." Blair slowed her pace and began to catch her breath.

"What happened there at the start of the race?" Steve asked.

"I got so excited—I decided to go for it! I thought maybe I could win my age group or something."

Steve found Blair's innocence endearing. "That would be something, wouldn't it? To win your age group in your first race, after training for a couple of months." He tried not to sound too judgmental.

Blair smiled. "I get it," she said between breaths. "I acted as though I were at the self-reliant achiever stage—starting up front, thinking I could outpace or at least keep pace with the best. I was at the classic enthusiastic beginner stage! So that's why I'm now at the disillusioned learner stage. It didn't take me long to get from D1 to D2, did it?" She clearly didn't need an answer.

Steve replied anyway. "Remember the old Italian proverb: Things get harder before they get easier." It struck him that he needed to heed the adage himself. His frustration with his job, he noted, was a normal part of the learning curve that needed to be acknowledged and dealt with. It wasn't a reason to quit.

Soon they passed the fountain and felt the invigorating spray. "I made that milestone," Blair panted. "Now what?"

"Keep going, one step at a time," Steve replied.

For the rest of the race, Blair asked Steve for the direction and support she needed. She encouraged herself out loud so Steve could add something if he thought she needed it. *Just make it around the corner. Good girl. Now just make it up to those two people—they don't seem that fast. Way to go, Blair!*

Every once in a while she asked Steve for specific directions. *Am I using my arms efficiently for uphill climbs? Do I need to do something different as we go downhill? If I'm breathing too hard to talk, does that mean I'm pacing myself too fast and should slow down?* Sometimes Steve gave her direct answers; sometimes he asked her to experience it and report back what she thought was best.

An hour into the race, Steve was jogging easily. Such was not the case for Blair. She was huffing and puffing, almost wheezing.

At last they caught sight of the finish line. "Okay, coach," Blair managed to pant, "other runners have said this was where they get that rush of adrenaline—their second wind—and sprint for the finish. I don't have any hope—I'm not sure I ever found my first wind. My legs are like lead. My lungs ache. I hope I can finish."

Steve was beginning to worry. He didn't want to carry her across. Then, they heard familiar voices cheering from the sidelines. They glanced over and saw a group of friends yelling and screaming like crazy.

"Oh, wow!" Blair said, "I didn't know they'd all be here!" She smiled despite the pain. "I'm sure they're in shock seeing that I'm still upright!"

"And that you're not last," Steve added.

With that, Blair's entire face and body changed. She caught her second wind. "Let's go!" she shouted, waving to their friends as she took off. Steve was just ready to kick it up a notch when he thought he noticed another familiar face in the crowd. Was that Cayla, cheering them on? No, it couldn't be. He looked again and the face was gone.

Blair beat him to the finish line. When he arrived, she hugged him jubilantly.

"Thank you, thank you, thank you!" she bubbled. He hugged back but kept her walking, fearing her legs might cramp.

"Look!" Blair said, pointing toward the finish line, "People are still finishing!"

People were still coming in, but even more runners had finished before them. It had taken them just over an hour to run 6.2 miles. That was not a fast time. At that moment Steve had an epiphany. He knew Blair was a very competitive person. Yet, curiously, knowing that hundreds of people had finished before she did didn't bother her. In fact, she was overjoyed to finish the race—to have achieved her goal. It didn't matter what the others had done.

The race helped Steve realize:

✳

*There is joy
in diagnosing your
development level
and getting the
direction and support
you need to achieve
your goal.*

✳

Without getting what she needed, Blair would have quit after the first two blocks. Just as he was about to quit after a couple of months of being an account executive.

Soon they were surrounded by their friends. They spent the next hour collecting their new T-shirts and enjoying the booths, exhibits, and goodies that came with finishing the race. As they walked to their cars, Blair hugged each of their friends.

"Thank you for giving me the support I needed, when I needed it," she said. Later, as they sat in the traffic line inching toward the parking lot attendant, Steve asked Blair to sort through the bag of coupons and free samples and find their parking ticket.

"Are you sure you put it in here?" she asked. "I can't find it."

They were at the parking lot pay booth. Steve hated holding up traffic. He rolled down the window to explain that they were still searching for the ticket. "Don't worry, it's taken care of," the attendant said.

"What do you mean?" Steve asked.

"That woman paid for you." The attendant pointed up ahead, where a small woman on a Harley-Davidson roared out the exit. "She said something about how special you are," the attendant said as he handed Steve a receipt.

Steve thanked the attendant, handed Blair the receipt, and pulled onto the highway. "That was Cayla up ahead," he said in an amazed tone of voice. "I thought I spotted her in the crowd, but figured I was seeing things."

"Did you tell her we'd be here?" Blair asked.

"I don't remember," Steve said.

"Well, this is no ordinary parking receipt," Blair said as she held it up for Steve to see. The receipt was emblazoned with the message:

> **The Third Trick of Self Leadership:**
> **BE PROACTIVE!**
> **GET WHAT YOU NEED**
> **TO SUCCEED!**

8

No Excuses

Steve was a man with a plan, out the door at 7:00 a.m. on Monday. First stop: Cayla's Café. Instead of beelining it for the coffee counter, he immediately looked around for Cayla and found her sitting at the same old table.

"You have a lot of explaining to do, Cayla."

"Do I?" she said, arching her brows.

"I don't want to sound ungrateful, but my curiosity is killing me."

A server began to bus the table next to them.

"Could you bring us a couple of coffees and a pair of scones?" Steve asked.

The server gave a distracted nod and walked away.

"Okay, back to the explanations," Steve said.

Cayla met his gaze. "I'm quite sure you have many legitimate questions, but don't you think we ought to focus on the most important questions first? How are you going to handle your lunch with Rhonda? How are you going to save your job? How are you going to implement the plan you and Blair put together?"

"See? That's what I mean!" Steve said in a rising voice. "How do you know Blair and I put a plan together?"

Cayla made a palm-down motion. "Calm yourself. I saw the two of you during the race. You are both very bright, so I just figured you would leverage your partnership and come up with a plan for today."

"Fine," said Steve. "Your great powers of observation and reasoning have worked again. But why were you there observing in the first place? I don't remember telling you about the race."

Again Cayla responded matter-of-factly. "I knew some other people in the race, and I was there to cheer them on. You might have noticed one of them—a wonderful lady. She's eighty-two and she's still running! Finished before the two of you, I might add."

"Glad Blair didn't notice that," Steve said under his breath.

"What was that?" Cayla asked.

"Nothing," Steve said with a half-smile. "I guess I jumped to conclusions. But you have to admit there have been an inordinate number of coincidences lately. Like our chance meeting near Hal's Harleys, for example."

"Life is full of pleasant surprises," Cayla said. "Look, you have only a few hours before your big meeting with Rhonda. What questions do you have about your plan?"

Steve pulled out the multipage plan that he and Blair had created and handed it to Cayla. It was then that he realized they hadn't gotten their coffee and scones. As the server walked by, Steve caught his attention.

"Excuse me," he said abruptly. "Is our order on the way?"

"I'll check," said the server as he walked off.

Cayla was still concentrating on the plan, making little noises in apparent approval. Steve decided that her "uh hum's" were not enough, and decided to ask for feedback.

"Since I'm at the D2–disillusioned learner stage as a self leader—especially when it comes to my meeting with Rhonda—is it okay to ask you for more specifics?"

Cayla didn't respond immediately. She seemed to be weighing his question.

Fearing he'd blundered, Steve stuttered, "If you can't, I mean, if you don't want to give me feedback—"

Cayla put her finger to her mouth. "Watch," she whispered.

As the server walked by again, Cayla reached out to get his attention. "Excuse me, Gary. I need to ask you about our order. My colleague here is getting grumpy without his morning java!" she said with a smile.

"Oh, I know the feeling! Let me check." The server turned around and hurried back to the coffee counter.

"Thank you!" Cayla called, oozing appreciation.

Gary returned a few seconds later with the coffee and scones.

"Must be your charming personality," Steve quipped. "He ignored me when I asked."

"Not charm—technique," Cayla explained. "I simply used the two most powerful words in the English language to get what I needed."

" 'Thank you'?" Steve ventured.

"That didn't hurt, I suppose. But that's not really what made the difference. What was different about the way you addressed Gary versus the way I handled the situation?"

Steve tried to think.

Cayla provided the answer. "I used the two most powerful words in the English language for getting cooperation."

Steve waited to hear what the two words were.

"*I need*," Cayla declared.

"That's it?"

"Correct," Cayla said firmly.

"That's interesting, Cayla, but what does that have to do with you giving me feedback?"

"It's not that I don't want to give you feedback, it's just that there is a much more powerful way for you to get feedback from me. Don't ask."

Now Steve was totally lost. "But I thought I should be proactive as a self leader and ask for feedback."

"I said *get* the feedback—I didn't say *ask* for it. Let me be more precise. Don't put the request in the form of a question. In this case, playing *Jeopardy!*® puts you in jeopardy." Cayla smiled at her play on words before reinforcing:

�֎

*"The two most
powerful words
to get what you need
to succeed are,
'I NEED.'"*

✖

"As a self leader, it is your responsibility to get the feedback, direction, and support you need," said Cayla. "The problem is that instead of stating what you need in a direct, forthright manner—especially when you are at the D2– disillusioned learner stage—you get trapped asking dumb questions."

"Like what?" Steve queried, fearing he'd just asked one.

"Here's a great example," Cayla said, full of enthusiasm. "A man got on the subway in New York City and discovered that there was only one seat left. But there was something on the seat that he didn't want on his slacks, so he laid his newspaper down and sat on it. A few moments later a woman tapped him on the shoulder and asked, 'Excuse me, sir, are you reading your newspaper?' The man thought that was one of the dumbest questions he'd ever heard. He couldn't help himself. He stood up, turned the page, sat back down on the paper, and replied, 'Yes ma'am, I am.' "

Cayla laughed at her story. "That's the problem with a dumb question. You get a dumb answer."

Steve cracked up—more at Cayla than at her story. But he wasn't sure about this question thing. How could he ask for help without asking a question? Steve took a risk.

"Cayla, I hope this isn't another dumb question. But what makes a question dumb? Obviously not all questions are dumb. In fact, I've always heard that there's no such thing as a dumb question."

"Smart question," Cayla said. "There are three types of dumb questions. One, when the answer is obvious. Two, when you're not willing to hear a certain response. And three, when you already know what you want to hear.

"For example, Rhonda is running around with her head cut off, but you need some help. So you ask, 'Are you busy?' That's a dumb question. Of course she's busy! So she says something like, 'There just aren't enough hours in the day.' You feel guilty, so you get flustered and leave her alone so as not to add to her burden.

"It is better for you to just simply state your needs truthfully: 'Rhonda, I need fifteen minutes of your time to discuss this project. If this isn't a good time, I can come back at three o'clock.' "

Steve couldn't deny that he often asked what appeared to be the dumb question instead of stating his needs directly. "What makes the 'I need' phrase so powerful?" he asked.

"When you tell someone you *want* something, their first thought is often, *We all want things we can't have*. When you use the *I need* phrase, you're coming from a position of strength. You've thought about what it's going to take to succeed and are requesting a person's help. It's amazing, but human beings love to feel needed. They love to think they can help you. 'I need' is very compelling."

"All right. I'll try not to ask dumb questions. But I reserve the right to ask smart ones," Steve said. "How's this: I *need* specific feedback on my plan so I can get what I need to make it work."

Cayla complied immediately by turning her attention to Steve's neatly printed plan. After reading it over, she summarized:

"You **challenge assumed constraints**, the first trick of self leadership, by listing potential and actual assumed constraints that could limit your success on the United Bank account. The way you flipped your assumed constraints is very effective—this one, for example: 'My assumed constraint is that I think Roger is egotistical and won't listen to anything I say.' The flipped statement: 'Roger is not egotistical and is open to my recommendations.'

"You **activate your points of power**, the second trick of self leadership, by highlighting your strengths and resources. But you've gone even one step further and identified other people who have points of power that you can draw upon as you implement your plan. You must feel good about that.

"And, finally, you have started using the third trick of self leadership—**be proactive to get what you need to succeed**—by prioritizing your most important goals on the United Bank account, diagnosing your development level on each of them, and determining the leadership style you need."

For the next hour, Cayla helped Steve create an agenda for his meeting with Rhonda. Finally, it was time for Steve to go. He packed up the papers and took a last swig of his now cold coffee. Before he left, Steve reached over and gave her a big hug.

"This meant a lot to me today. I won't forget it—no matter what happens." Cayla was visibly moved. She squeezed his arm and headed for her office. As Steve walked out the door, he heard her voice calling out:

"Don't get derailed by disillusionment!"

Steve smiled. Cayla always seemed to have the last word.

Time to work the magic, Steve thought.

He straightened his already straight tie and glanced in the rearview mirror to get a sense of himself before going into Irma's Eatery. He was a few minutes early. The last thing he wanted to do was keep Rhonda waiting.

Briefcase in hand, he found the most private booth available and faced forward so he could catch Rhonda's attention when she entered. He pulled out his laptop and reviewed his notes on the United Bank proposal. The waitress dropped off a glass of ice water.

"Thanks, Tina. I need another glass—someone will be joining me for lunch." Steve smiled at how well the little things worked. Tina was not only prompt, but attentive.

"Looks like an important meeting," Tina observed.

"Could be one of the most important in my career so far, as a matter of fact," Steve said.

"Is there anything I can do to make it go more smoothly?"

"Wow, that's really kind of you. Come to think of it, yes. If this is too much to ask, let me know. I need to stay focused, so I'd appreciate it if rather than checking in on how we're doing and risk interrupting a delicate moment, you wait for me to signal that we need something. Oh, and make sure you give the check to me."

"Consider it done." Tina gave the thumbs-up sign. "And good luck!"

Steve smiled. It felt good to be proactive about getting what he needed to succeed.

Outside the window, a silver-gray BMW pulled into the parking lot. He watched as Rhonda gathered her things and made her way to the restaurant's entrance. Confident and poised, Rhonda was someone Steve admired on general principle. He prepared himself for her direct, no-nonsense approach. She would pull no punches, get right to the point, and leave with a general plan of action. As nervous as he was, he realized how much he wanted to work with her—he had so much to learn.

He stood so she could spot him. She smiled. He observed that the smile was genuine but restrained. He understood that she needed to hold back, given the seriousness of the situation.

Steve stepped out of the booth to greet her. They did a semiprofessional half-handshake, half-hug hello. After Rhonda sat, so did Steve.

Typically, Steve would wait for Rhonda to speak. He would listen, formulate an opinion, and then decide how or whether to respond. But this was a time to be bold, so before Rhonda began, Steve launched the first volley.

"Rhonda, I know you cut your trip short because of this meeting. You expressed disappointment that you heard about the outcome of the presentation from Roger and United Bank before you heard from me. I'm not going to give you excuses. I think your disappointment is warranted. I'm here to bring you up to speed with what I know and listen to what you think. But, I also need you to know that I've done my homework. I have ideas for moving forward and I trust you'll be open to discussing them."

"What kind of ideas?" Rhonda asked.

"I've got a two-pronged approach. One is a strategy for communicating with Roger and rescuing the ad campaign. Obviously, that is the most pressing concern for you and Creative Advertising. The second approach is a plan for the way you and I should collaborate going forward. I didn't realize until this past week that I need direction and support from you and others to do my job effectively while I'm on the learning curve. I plan to be much more proactive in the future to get what I need to succeed—and not let you or the agency down."

Rhonda took a moment before replying. "There's no doubt the United Bank account is in crisis," she said. "If I had a dollar for every time we've had to rally to save a client, I could retire. I need to get your update, but I'm confident we can save this one," Rhonda said.

Steve heaved a silent sigh of relief. Losing his job would have been bad enough, but the guilt from losing the account would have made it worse. He was reaching for the proposal to begin filling Rhonda in, but she wasn't finished.

"Frankly, Steve, I am more worried about you. I know how conscientious you are about your work, and the pride you take in doing good work. I don't want to lose you, but I feel you slipping away."

Steve could barely take it in. She was afraid of losing *him*? He blurted out what could have been the dumbest question he'd ever asked.

"You mean you aren't going to fire me?"

To his astonishment, Rhonda laughed. "I'm sorry," Rhonda said, trying to control her amusement. "I remember hearing a story—who knows if it's true, but it's a great story—about Tom Watson, the legendary leader of IBM. A young man sent to Watson's office was terrified because he'd been in charge of a project that had lost thousands of dollars—maybe millions. The number goes up every time I hear the story. Anyway, the young man went into this intimidating office and Watson said, 'Tell me what happened, what you learned; what went right, what went wrong.' So for an hour the young man spilled his guts, told Watson everything he thought was relevant. At the end of the meeting Watson thanked the young man and shook his hand. The young man sat there stunned and asked the same question you just asked me—'You're not going to fire me?' You know what Watson said?"

Steve shook his head. "What?"

"Story has it that Watson bellowed, 'Fire you? I just spent thousands of dollars training you, why would I fire you?' " Rhonda laughed her hearty, full-throated laugh. "Steve, I'm in the same boat as Watson. I figure you've learned more in the last week than any MBA program could teach. I can't afford to fire you!"

Not one to trust good news immediately, Steve had one more issue to raise. "I heard rumors that you were going to replace me with Grant on the account."

Rhonda screwed up her face in a look Steve couldn't decipher. He waited for her to respond. Finally she said, "Remember the children's game of telephone, where one kid whispered a message in another's ear, and that kid passed it to the next kid, and by the time the message got back around it was a total distortion of the original message?"

"So what was the original message?" Steve asked.

"It wasn't a message; it was just an idea I was considering. Grant has real potential and wonderful people skills, but he lacks focus and attention to detail—the very qualities you have in spades. My thought was to have him become your junior account executive so you could teach him a wider variety of skills."

Steve felt like jumping for joy. "Well, if you're not firing me, and I'm not quitting, I guess we've got a lot of work to do. And I obviously have a lot to learn before I start mentoring Grant. Let's order lunch and I'll show you my plans." Steve signaled Tina, who was on the spot in a second.

As they ate, Steve showed the United Bank proposal to Rhonda, explaining why he thought the client rejected the budget, production plan, and creative approach. "I was a master budget and schedule-maker when I assisted you, but I didn't—I don't—know how to gather the right information and get by-in from the client. Those were your responsibilities that I never learned to do."

Steve had decided to avoid using the D-laden language of the Situational Leadership® II Model. The model would guide his thoughts and comments, though he feared it would confuse things to speak a language Rhonda didn't know. But as he shared his insights he remembered how much easier it had been to communicate with Blair when they both spoke the language. So he pulled out the model and gave Rhonda a brief overview.

Rhonda was more than receptive. She asked for specific examples. Steve pulled out the sheet where he had prioritized his goals, diagnosed his development level on each, and determined the leadership style he needed. He explained to Rhonda that she wasn't the only one he would rely on for leadership.

"I've challenged the assumed constraints I had about my team and the client. I've also activated my points of power and come to realize there are many people and resources available to me. In other words, you're not the only one who can lead me."

Rhonda seemed relieved that the responsibility was not entirely hers. "So you're saying,

✻

*A leader is
anyone who
can give you the
support and direction
you need
to achieve
your goal."*

✻

"That's right!" Steve said brightly. "But as my coach, boss, and, right now, savior of the United Bank account, I need as much direction as I can get from you."

"Well, here it comes," Rhonda warned. "The reason this presentation failed is because you focused on what you were comfortable with and missed the point. You attempted to use the budget and production schedule to drive the strategy. It's got to be the other way around. Strategic approach first, then creative, then budgets and schedules. You went with what you knew, but in this case it took you in the wrong direction. That's why Peter and Alexa couldn't come up with anything creative. They were working in a vacuum."

"But I couldn't get the client to come up with or agree on strategy," Steve groaned.

"Steve, I'm going to turn your model upside down on you here. Has United Bank ever mounted a full-blown ad campaign before? Have they ever worked with an ad agency, let alone our ad agency, before? Are Roger and his reps advertising experts?"

Steve looked at Rhonda, to the model, and back to Rhonda as the realization hit him. He had abandoned United Bank just as he'd felt Rhonda had abandoned him. They didn't have a clue how to give him a strategy.

"Talk about the blind leading the blind," Steve conceded. "They were enthusiastic beginners at D1 and now I'm sure they are disillusioned learners at D2 on the entire process. We need to give them high direction and high support to get buy-in for the strategy."

"Let's get together tomorrow afternoon and I'll help you work on the strategy," said Rhonda.

They pulled out their phones and scheduled a meeting.

At Steve's signal, Tina slipped him the check and a questioning look. She motioned, *Thumbs-up or thumbs-down?* Steve replied with an under-the-table double thumbs-up. In a quiet voice he said, "Thanks for your graciousness, and keep the change." He gave her a wink and a generous tip.

9

One Minute Magic

Steve stood behind the stage, speaking softly to the audiovisual technician through his headset. He was again the coproducer of this year's advertising awards program. The master of ceremonies announced the next category: Best of Show for overall advertising campaign. As the five finalists were read, Steve peeked out at the audience. Rhonda and Grant were sitting in the third row with Roger from United Bank. Steve hoped they wouldn't be too disappointed.

The MC opened the envelope. "The winner is"—he paused—"Irma's Italian Eateries!" A whoop went up from the crowd as the names of the creative team and ad agency were announced.

Steve watched Rhonda reach over and give Roger a consoling pat on the arm. *Just wait*, he thought.

The MC handed out the triangular-shaped crystal trophies and waited for the applause to wind down before making the next announcement. "This year the panel of judges added a new category—the Judges' Award for Best of Show among new advertisers. And that award goes to— United Bank!"

Steve watched Roger jump up from his seat and grab Grant by the shoulders. Steve laughed out loud at seeing the staid bank president so animated. Roger had turned out to be an ideal client. As the MC recognized Creative Advertising and the United Bank team, Steve found himself happier for the others than for himself: Peter for art direction, Alexa for copywriting, Maril for media buying, Jude for production, Grant as junior account executive, and Steve as account executive. The proud-mama look on Rhonda's face was priceless.

The nine months since Rhonda and Steve met at Irma's Eatery had been intense. It was only fitting that the restaurant chain should win the big award and that Creative Advertising should win the surprise award of the evening. Steve was grateful to Rhonda and his team, but also to his two best collaborators for success—Blair and Cayla. Blair had grown from girlfriend to wife and from struggling runner to marathoner, trusting the Situational Leadership® II Model to help her master long-distance running and their new marriage. Steve continued to be mentored by Cayla, though not as frequently as in the beginning. Steve felt a pang of sadness—there was no Cayla sighting this night. He had become used to his favorite magician popping up at the strangest yet most appropriate times.

Steve tied up loose ends backstage, thanked the MC for a job well done, and joined the small group of people still chatting in the lobby. They broke into applause as he walked in. There were bear hugs and pats on the back from coworkers, colleagues, friends, and, of course, Blair. Suddenly Steve felt a tug at his arm. It was Rhonda.

Pulling him aside, she cupped her hand over his ear and whispered, "Meet me in my office first thing Monday morning." She smiled and was off.

On Monday, Steve greeted Phyllis—who was now his secretary as well as Rhonda's. "The boss wants to see me. Any idea why?"

Smiling her Mona Lisa smile, Phyllis refused to divulge anything.

Hearing Steve's voice, Rhonda came out to usher him into her office. "Steve," she said as she shut the door, "I ran an idea past Roger, and he's in agreement pending your input. I want to pull you off United Bank and promote Grant to account executive."

Steve didn't respond, hoping there was more to the story. Rhonda took it as a sign to continue. "I want to promote you to head of the new business development department. If we land an account that is especially attractive to you, you have the option to take it on as an account executive. What do you think?"

Steve processed the news for a moment before saying, "The idea intrigues me. My concern is that I'd leave a position where I'm at the self-reliant achiever–D4 stage on most of my goals for a position where I'm at the enthusiastic beginner–D1 stage on almost every goal. It's not only a new position for me, but for the agency."

"That's why we want you," Rhonda said emphatically. "The role needs someone who will shape it. Someone who will challenge the assumed constraint that 'it's never been done before.' Someone who will activate points of power to draw upon resources such as me and my partners who have been responsible for new business since we started the company. Someone who knows how to get the direction and support they need to succeed in the role."

Steve was flattered—especially after Rhonda alluded to salary and benefit increases. Still—not motivated by money, power, or status and never one to make snap decisions— Steve told Rhonda he'd give her an answer the next day.

Steve would talk it over with Blair. But he also felt honor-bound to share the decision with his mentor.

Steve parked directly in front of Cayla's Café. It had been weeks since he'd had a chance to visit her and sip a mocha. The familiar door chime announced his arrival. He checked out their regular table and, to his surprise, saw Cayla sitting with a jovial-looking fellow who seemed somehow vaguely familiar. When Cayla spotted Steve, she smiled and waved.

"Come here!" she called. "I have someone I'd like you to meet."

Steve walked over and extended his hand to the familiar stranger. "Hi, I'm Steve," he said.

The man gave Steve an earnest handshake. "Pleased to meet you, Steve. I'm—"

"The one-and-only One Minute Manager!" Cayla chimed in. "This is the guy who taught me everything I know about the magic of self leadership."

Steve's face lit up. "Wow! It's great to meet you," he said. "I can't tell you how much your teaching has changed my life for the better."

The One Minute Manager smiled humbly. "I feel as though I know you. Cayla has told me all about you. You should feel very proud."

Steve smiled. "When I tell her the latest good news, Cayla's the one who'll feel proud. I also need her advice about an offer my boss made me. But wait, I'm interrupting you. I'll be glad to come back later."

"Ha!" The One Minute Manager let out a hearty laugh. "How can you refuse him, Cayla? He used the 'I need' phrase."

Cayla laughed and signaled Steve to sit down. Steve told them about United Bank's win at the ad awards program and his pride for his team's success. Then he outlined his new job opportunity.

"Congratulations, Steve." Cayla turned to the One Minute Manager and said, "I guess it's time."

"Time for what?" Steve asked apprehensively.

"To let you go," Cayla responded.

Steve looked to her, then to the One Minute Manager, for an explanation.

"Steve," he said, "the beauty of developing a self leader is that it ultimately frees managers to focus their attention where it's most needed. Cayla's job was to teach you how to be a self leader. She accomplished her goal. It's time she turned her attention to others who need her."

"But I'm not at the self-reliant achiever level on everything. I still need direction and support," Steve protested.

"You may not be at the self-reliant achiever level on many of the goals and tasks required in your new job opportunity," the One Minute Manager said firmly, "but you've mastered the three tricks of self leadership:

✻

*Self leaders
challenge assumed constraints,
activate their points of power,
and are proactive about getting
what they need to succeed.*

✻

"Just continue to practice the tricks and you'll manage yourself to success. There are other would-be self leaders who need Cayla now," he said.

The café door burst open and a gaggle of children rushed in, heading straight for Cayla's Magic Corner.

"Uh-oh!" Cayla said as she jumped from her chair. "Showtime!"

"Cayla," Steve said as he grabbed her elbow, "before you go, how can I thank you? How can I ever repay you for your help?"

"Just be yourself," Cayla responded.

Before Steve could say more, Cayla was in front of the eager children, perched on her stool, looking intently at each one of them as she gained their attention. In her rich voice she said, "My name is Cayla, and I am a magician."

When the applause subsided, Cayla glanced at Steve as she asked the spellbound children, "Do you believe in magic?"

Steve smiled. *What do you know—I do believe in magic*, he thought. At that moment, he felt a tap on his shoulder.

"Good on you!" the One Minute Manager whispered into his ear. "You'll make a fine magician."

"What do you mean?" Steve whispered back.

The One Minute Manager simply pointed to a forlorn-looking woman sitting alone at a table. With her faraway stare, she looked as Steve must have looked when he first met Cayla.

The One Minute Manager winked and rose from his seat, heading for the exit.

As he watched the One Minute Manager disappear through the door, Steve suddenly knew how he would thank Cayla. He wouldn't do it by repaying her directly. He would thank her by carrying on the legacy of the One Minute Manager and

✸

Teach others
the magic
of self leadership

✸

Appendix: The Business Card Trick

Can you cut a hole from a business card large enough to stick your head through? This trick demonstrates the power of challenging assumed constraints. To master it, follow these four steps:

1. Take a business card and fold it in half lengthwise. Starting from the folded edge, cut a series of slits one-quarter inch apart to within about one-half inch of the opposite side.

2. Turn the card completely around so that the open edges are facing you. Between the slits, cut more slits going in the opposite direction, stopping about one-half inch from the opposite end of the card.

3. Slip the scissors into the fold starting after the first slit. Cut along the folded edge, stopping at the last slit, being careful to leave one-quarter inch of the fold intact at each end.

4. Carefully unfold the card, pulling the slits apart as wide as they will go, and slip the paper ring over your head.

Acknowledgments

We would like to thank the people who have brought their own special magic to this book: **Martha Lawrence**, who not only helped shape this book but our hearts as well; our new SSL team members Victoria Cutler, Kim King, and Jay Campbell; **Maril Adrian**, who shepherded Self Leadership and the EDGE to their success; **Linda Hulst**, **Patrice DeVeau Simpson**, and **Charlene Ables**, who took personal interest in improving the quality of this book; clients and colleagues who took time from their busy lives to provide feedback and support, especially **The Marmaxx Group** and **Nancy Maher**; **Jim Martin** of Dow Chemical; **Humberto Medina**, **Trevor Keighly**, **Linda Taylor**, **Carla de Bose**, **Jason Arnold**, **Richard Andrews**, **Debra Talbert**, and **Mark Manning** of The Ken Blanchard Companies; and our brilliant editor at William Morrow, **Henry Ferris**.

Susan: I would like to personally thank **Kenny Taylor**, who teaches wisdom through the martial arts and self leadership through application; **Peter Turner**, who taught me to take magic seriously; **Bill Brown**, who opened my eyes to things unseen; **Aubrey Keen**, who has partnered with me in my ongoing search for self-knowledge; **Kip Woodring**, for his support over many years, his motorcycling wisdom, and his classic parts-salesman song.

We all wish to thank our partners. Ken thanks his wife, **Margie**, who has been an inspiration and learning partner for more than fifty years. Susan thanks **Drea Zigarmi**, her mentor and life partner, whose passion about leadership is exceeded only by his passion for good thinking; Laurence thanks **Laurie Ozanne Hawkins**, who has been part of the Blanchard journey all the way.

About the Authors

Ken Blanchard is the chief spiritual officer of The Ken Blanchard Companies, a worldwide human resource development company. He is also cofounder of Lead Like Jesus, a global leadership development organization that helps individuals and organizations lead more effectively by following the model of Jesus. Few people have made a more positive and lasting impact on the day-to-day management of people and companies as Ken Blanchard. He is the author of several best-selling books, including the blockbuster international bestseller *The One Minute Manager* and the giant business bestsellers *Leadership and the One Minute Manager, Raving Fans,* and *Gung Ho!*. His books have combined sales of more than twenty million copies in more than forty languages. He and his wife, Margie, live in San Diego and work with their son Scott, daughter Debbie, and Scott's wife, Madeleine.

Susan Fowler has been a consulting partner with The Ken Blanchard Companies since 1990. With Ken Blanchard and Laurence Hawkins she created—and is the lead developer of—Self Leadership, considered one of the best programs in the world promoting proactive workplace behaviors. She is also the lead developer of the Optimal Motivation training experience and author of the bestselling book *Why Motivating People Doesn't Work... And What Does: The New Science of Leading, Energizing, and Engaging.* During her thirty-year career she has published bylined articles, peer-reviewed research, and books including *Achieve Leadership Genius* with Drea Zigarmi and Dick Lyles, *Leading at a Higher Level* with Ken Blanchard, *The Team Leader's Idea-a-Day Guide* with Drea Zigarmi, *Empowerment* with Ken Blanchard, *Good Leaders, Good Shepherds* with Dick Lyles, as well as audio programs on *Mentoring: How to Foster Your Career's Most Crucial Relationships* and *Overcoming Procrastination.*

Susan is one of the foremost experts on personal empowerment in the world today, having spoken in all fifty states in the U.S. and more than twenty foreign countries. In 2002 she received a lifetime achievement award for creative instructional design from Thiagi's North American Simulation and Gaming Association. She received her bachelor of science degree in business from the University of Colorado at Boulder and is currently an adjunct professor for the University of San Diego's masters of science in Executive Leadership degree program.

Laurence Hawkins is an internationally renowned management consultant and trainer and a dynamic motivational speaker. For the past twenty years he has worked with hundreds of organizations in the areas of leadership training, motivation, team building, and organizational development.

His international experience has won him consulting and training contracts in South America, the Far East, and several European countries, including Spain, England, Italy, Sweden, Holland, and Denmark. Domestically and internationally, he has earned the reputation of being a dedicated and well-versed professional who inspires positive results in a practical manner.

Laurence's client list includes a variety of industries and such corporate giants as Lockheed Martin, AT&T, Johnson & Johnson, and Bristol-Meyers Squibb, as well as a number of schools, hospitals, restaurants, and start-ups.

With Ken Blanchard and Susan Fowler, he coauthored the Self Leadership program, which focuses on empowerment and taking initiative when you're not in charge.

Laurence received his bachelor's degree in American history and literature from Williams College and his master's and doctorate degrees in leadership and organizational behavior from the University of Massachusetts, Amherst.

Services Available

Self Leadership and the One Minute Manager completes the trilogy that started with *Leadership and the One Minute Manager*, followed by *The One Minute Manager Builds High Performing Teams*. These three books describe the three leadership programs that have played a major role in building The Ken Blanchard Companies®.

Our company is committed to helping leaders and organizations perform at a higher level. The concepts and beliefs presented in this book are just a few of the ways that Ken, his company, and Blanchard International—a global network of world-class consultants, trainers, and coaches—have helped organizations improve workplace productivity, employee satisfaction, and customer loyalty around the world.

If you would like additional information about how to apply these concepts and approaches in your organization, or if you would like information on other services, programs, and products offered by Blanchard International, please contact us at

The Ken Blanchard Companies
World Headquarters
125 State Place
Escondido, California 92029
United States
Phone: +1-760-489-5005
E-mail: International@kenblanchard.com
Website: www.kenblanchard.com

Situational Leadership® II Model

Leadership Styles

HIGH

SUPPORTIVE BEHAVIOR

S3
High Supportive and Low Directive Behavior

SUPPORTING

S2
High Directive and High Supportive Behavior

COACHING

S4
Low Supportive and Low Directive Behavior

DELEGATING

S1
High Directive and Low Supportive Behavior

DIRECTING

LOW — DIRECTIVE BEHAVIOR ⟶ HIGH

D4
High Competence
—•—
High Commitment

D3
Moderate to High Competence
—•—
Variable Commitment

D2
Low to Some Competence
—•—
Low Commitment

D1
Low Competence
—•—
High Commitment

DEVELOPED ⟵ DEVELOPING

Development Levels